C. S. LEWIS EXPLORES VICE *and* VIRTUE

GERARD REED

Beacon Hill Press of Kansas City
Kansas City, Missouri

Copyright 2001
by Beacon Hill Press of Kansas City

ISBN 083-411-8947

Printed in the
United States of America

Cover Design: Ted Ferguson

Library of Congress Cataloging-in-Publication Data

Reed, Gerard.
    C. S. Lewis explores vice and virtue / Gerard Reed.
      p. cm.
    Includes bibliographical references.
    ISBN 0-8341-1894-7
     1. Deadly sins. 2. Cardinal virtues. 3. Lewis, C. S. (Clive Staples), 1898-1963. I. Title.

BV4626 .R44 2001
241'.3—dc21

                                   2001025401

10   9   8   7   6   5   4   3   2   1

To my students
at Southern Nazarene University,
MidAmerica Nazarene University,
and Point Loma Nazarene University,
who over many years have challenged and
blessed me by granting me the
privilege of serving as their professor.

Contents

Preface

THROUGHOUT THE LAST CENTURY, scores of analysts warned that Western civilization was collapsing like a wounded warrior before a resurgent barbarism. This stands revealed in such items as a controversial art exhibit in Brooklyn that featured animal parts in formaldehyde and a portrait of the Virgin Mary covered with elephant dung.

As a result, much has been written prescribing a restoration of traditional virtues. Underlying much of this is a pivotal work by one of the world's finest ethicists, Alastair MacIntyre, who thinks the world's fate, humanity's well-being, rests in the balance. He suspects that our era resembles the era marking the transition from the ancient to the medieval world, an era of "barbarism and darkness."[1] In our day, he says, "the barbarians are not waiting beyond the frontiers; they have already been governing us from quite some time."[2]

Evangelical theologian David Wells shares MacIntyre's concern and addressed it in *Losing Our Virtue: Why the Church Must Recover Its Moral Vision.* He addresses "the disintegrating moral culture in American society and what this now means for the Church,"[3] endorsing Judge Robert Bork's lament that "the traditional virtues of this culture are being lost, its vices multiplied, its values degraded—in short, the culture itself is unraveling."[4]

We've lost our moral compass. Wells says, "Functionally, we are not morally disengaged, adrift, and alienated; we are morally obliterated. We are, in practice, not only moral illiterati; we have become morally vacant."[5] Quite an indictment! Sadly, rather than manning the outposts and barricades in the culture war, many Evangelical churches have retreated into the shadows. They have tolerated "an erosion of character to the point that today, no discernible ethical differences are evident in behavior when those claiming to have been reborn and secularists are compared."[6]

The "classical spirituality" that sustained earlier generations focused on God's holiness. Love and compassion were highlighted within the context of God's character: holiness. Conforming to the truth, becoming holy, was the believer's true vocation. But few churches today stress holiness. Doctrines such as God's wrath, judgment, and moral requirements remain unmentioned lest they offend folks in the pews.

"Tolerance," an essentially pagan virtue, has been deftly interwoven into Christian thought (edging aside forgiveness) and has been elevated into the central mark of goodness. Almighty God is often portrayed as a forever forgiving, perennially permissive "Abba" who demands nothing from His children.

As a result, sin is defined in psychological rather than ethical terms—it's a problem we have dealing with ourselves rather than God. Sin is wrong, we're told, because it harms *us*—not because it offends God. So we rarely repent of our transgressions. Instead, we admit our inner turmoil, reveal our problems and frustrations, and imagine that God is a loving psychic healer anxious to comfort us. Self-sacrifice has been discarded in favor of self-realization. Self-denial and self-discipline have been storehoused so that physical and psychological health can be marketed.

While Wells's litany about our predicament might tempt us to despair, he proposes two remedies. First, we must proclaim the truth about sin. "Without an understanding of sin—sin understood within a powerfully conceived moral vision of reality—there can be no deep believing of the Gospel. This, then, is not an optional task but an essential and inescapable one."[7]

Second, the Church must clean house. Christians must be virtuous, holy people. The world simply dismisses much of the God talk that pervades the airwaves. Evangelicals, especially, must live ethically. And this is possible within the provisions of grace. "Scripture is clear in its teaching that the 'old man,' who has lived comfortably in the fallen world, must die with its entire understanding of the self and its relationship to God, if the 'new man' is to emerge in Christ."[8]

So the Church must preach the Word. The Word, however, is not simply an announcement that "all is forgiven." It calls us to repentance, to holiness. We can be redeemed only as we recover the deeply moral truth found in the Word. And only as we are redeemed and live the moral implications of that redemption can we offer hope and guidance to a world in chaos.

In *The Death of Character*, James Davison Hunter adds important data to MacIntyre's indictment. Character in America has collapsed, he thinks, because the dogmatic creeds undergirding it have been discarded. The theological foundation, the religious worldview, that made possible the cultivation of moral character no longer shapes America's culture. We're suffocating in the spineless slime left by earlier generations; "We want the flower of moral seriousness to blossom, but we have pulled the plant up by its roots."[9]

Revealingly, we hear much talk about the need for "values," the restoration of "values." But values are human measures we place on things—just as we price goods in the grocery store. "Values are truths that have been deprived of their commanding character. They are substitutes for revelation, imperatives that have dissolved into a range of possibilities. The very word 'value' signifies the reduction of truth to utility, taboo to fashion, conviction to mere preference; all provisional, all exchangeable. Both values and 'lifestyle'—a way of living that reflects that accumulation of one's values—bespeak a world in which nothing is sacred."[10]

The death of character, strangely enough, has been aided by the very people who claim to desire character—the "moral education establishment, those who have given their professional life to the task of moral education."[11] These people, usually with the best intentions, have effectively sterilized the soil needed for the plants they want to flourish. Hunter argues that our public schools and other institutions (including churches) entrusted with educating our children have embraced strategies that "aggravate rather than ameliorate the problem. Rather than restore character and its attending moral ideals, they are complicit in destroying them."[12] He says,

> We say we want a renewal of character in our day but we don't really know what we ask for. To have a renewal of character is to have a renewal of a creedal order that constrains, limits, binds, obligates and compels. This price is too high for us to pay. We want character but without unyielding conviction; we want strong morality but without the emotional burden of guilt or shame; we want virtue but without particular moral justifications that invariably offend; we want good without having to name evil; we want decency

without the authority to insist upon it; we want moral community without any limitations to personal freedom. In short, we want what we cannot possibly have on terms that we want it.[13]

Hunter says that few Americans really want to hear what we must do. We must again make theology central to a counterculture that derives its moral truths from a transcendent God. Adults, especially, must teach and live by a divine law, even if it's not "acceptable" to everyone. Strong communities of faith incubate character. In time, perhaps, such small communities could shape a culture of character we so clearly need. The deepest struggle in North America is not about art or abortion but of beliefs. A "cosmic struggle" pits Christians against secularists, theists against naturalists. Christians must live the truths revealed to them through God's Word. To do so, we need help and wisdom to know "how then should we live."

C. S. Lewis provides us with one of the best bridges between the world we live in, so often lacking direction, and the classical world, which frequently offers us the best guidance. In an end-of-the-century piece published in 1999, *Christianity Today* reported a poll showing that America's Evangelicals ranked C. S. Lewis as the most influential writer of the century. Lists of the century's best books, whether compiled by Christian magazines or secular journals, placed Lewis's books (especially *Mere Christianity*) near the top. In 1996 John Stackhouse Jr. reviewed the most influential books published since World War II and noted that Lewis's books "indisputably affected American evangelicals during this period more than any of the other authors mentioned."[14]

Chuck Colson, founder of Prison Fellowship, is one of the world's outstanding Christian leaders. In an essay titled "The Oxford Prophet," he portrayed Lewis as "a true prophet for our postmodern age."[15] He was such a prophetic thinker, Colson suggests, because he was so immersed in history that he could critique "the narrow confines of the world-view of his own age."[16] Primarily, Lewis thought and wrote from what he called "the great body of Christian thought down through the ages."[17]

Prophets, by definition, address their world with a Word from God. And they usually speak in strong, if not stridently, moral terms. They castigate sin and call for sanctity. They indict vice and inculcate virtue. They're essential for any good society.

C. S. Lewis defended those "permanent things" that were foundational to thinkers such as Aristotle and Aquinas. So I try to use him as a *via media* between classical culture and modernity. I began to think about "vice and virtue in C. S. Lewis" while working on a book titled *C. S. Lewis and the Bright Shadow of Holiness*. Since holiness was so important to Lewis, it's understandable that he would routinely deal with ethical questions, for the holy life is the righteous life, the moral life, the ethical life.

However, we must always place the theological before the ethical. *Who* a person is, by God's grace, precedes what he or she does. Inner transformation precedes outer action. So this book should be considered as simply an aspect of Lewis's understanding of Christian theology.

In dealing with Lewis, I've tried to correctly understand and represent his views, fully aware that he never wrote a full-fledged ethical treatise. Nor did he ever put together the seven deadly sins and seven virtues, as did his medieval masters. So I have often drawn upon thinkers Lewis used, such as Aristotle and Aquinas, as well as added both personal anecdotes and other materials that seem relevant.

I am indebted to The Wesley Center at Point Loma Nazarene University for assistance in researching and writing this book.

Introduction
A "Middle-aged Moralist"

Truth is always about something,
but reality is that about which truth is.[1]

Most of us admire "moral" people, though this admiration is often akin to the applause portly fans give well-trained athletes. But then we easily turn around and condemn "moralists" and "moralistic" judgments. We can safely admire holy exemplars, such as Mother Teresa, from afar, and by voicing admiration we hope to reflect their luster. But we often dismiss calls to holy living as legalistic or self-righteous.

When scoffers ridiculed the Moral Majority organization in the 1980s, we saw that moralists—those who study and seek to teach morals—easily upset us, for they dare to assert that we, too, should be moral. So it's revealing that C. S. Lewis, lecturing at the University of London, labeled himself a "middle-aged moralist,"[2] accurately portraying a man whose writings reveal a sustained concern for righteousness.

Lewis believed great moralists simply remind us of "the primeval moral platitudes" we so routinely ignore. He saw himself as a spokesman for the *philosophia perennis*—the perennial philosophy shaped by Greek philosophers such as Plato and Aristotle, by medieval theologians such as Augustine and Thomas Aquinas, and by Anglicans such as Richard Hooker and Samuel Johnson. These thinkers blended moral realism, natural law, divine law, and the ethics of virtue into the central ethical tradition of Western civilization.

Though he was anything but a "legalist," Lewis the "moralist" insisted that righteousness is real, recognizable, and teachable. And he not only thought in moral terms but also was a moral person. His discerning contemporary Malcolm Muggeridge praised Lewis's integrity—a goodness "in his innermost being. His teaching and his writing were his *opus dei.*"[3]

Walter Hooper, an Anglican priest who spent many hours

13

with Lewis during his final years, concluded that "no matter how long I lived, no matter who else I met, I should never be in the company of such a supremely good human being again."[4]

The last essay Lewis wrote was for the *Saturday Evening Post*. He had been asked to write about sex, for the magazine's editors thought his other writings suitably "paradoxical" to elicit reader interest. When Nevill Coghill, Lewis's close friend, teased him about being able to invent sufficient "paradoxes" for the American public, Lewis said he merely repeated some of his mother's admonitions, teasing out a few of his own observations, "and this" struck the Americans as "outrageously paradoxical, *avant-garde* stuff."[5]

Lewis's article on sex probably proved more "paradoxical" than the *Saturday Evening Post* editors envisioned, for he titled it "We Have No Right to Happiness" and championed, like a chivalrous knight, the classical Christian virtue of chastity. More deeply, however, he ended his essay—his last words to the world—by condemning the creeping excesses of our sensate culture. If each of us composes his or her own bill of rights, claiming "rights" to collect undeserved dividends and indulge in unlimited pleasures, he warned, we will slide into a world in which everyone will insist on his or her own way and implode the common culture so carefully constructed by our forebears.

The Times Demand Some "Moralists"

Lewis's fears that Western civilization was collapsing partially explain his pugnacious "moralist" stance, for he wanted to battle for truth and justice, preserving the culture forged in Europe's centuries-long struggle with barbarism. People were not more evil, nor deeds more dastardly, than ever before. Rather, more alarmingly, people refused to judge them wrong. When increasing numbers of persons will not recognize that right is right, urging instead that everyone do whatever "feels" good, moralists must speak up.

Like a skilled prosecutor probing for evidence, Lewis unmasked the culture of modernism, exposing it as a perversion of Western Christian culture. Most of all, modernism lacks the commonsense sanity of the perennial philosophy best espoused by Aristotle and Thomas Aquinas—the position that goodness actually resides in an objective reality we can rationally apprehend and acquire.[6]

According to Lewis, though Scripture reminds us that our "righteousness is as filthy rags," this ought not dissuade us from forming moral standards. We may not attain perfection, but that's no excuse for easing off on the oars, refusing to exert our moral muscles. Lest we slip into the shelter of subjectivism, perhaps modernity's most deadly carcinogen, more destructive than DDT, we must remember that a real world surrounds us, packed with moral truths, and we can know it, at least in part.

Thinking, not feeling, once set moral standards. Yet today's propagandists urge us to adopt a new morality, a self-esteem-filled, feel-good morality. In Lewis's view, "Out of this apparently innocent idea comes the disease that will certainly end our species (and, in my view, damn our souls) if it is not crushed; the fatal superstition that men can create values, that a community can choose its 'ideology' as men choose their clothes."[7]

Many people condemn mass murder when condemning Hitler and Stalin, but then refuse to apply strict standards to themselves or their neighbors. But "unless the measuring rod is independent of the things measured, we can do no measuring."[8]

Lewis strongly opposed the "man is the measure" relativism so evident today. "Everything's relative," people say, as if they were accurately reciting Einstein's famous theorem. We're told that we all have different value systems, with none being right or wrong. We're widely urged in schools and churches to offer our opinions—as if hearing each other's opinions would magically resolve issues. Instead, like amateur carpenters building a house without blueprints, we all construct our own version of reality and air our opinions.

Amazingly, in today's colleges and universities many students parrot skeptical professors and declare, after four years of study, that all they've learned is that they *know* nothing. They say what's truly important is endlessly asking questions and searching—never grasping—permanent truths. They're on a journey, they declare, a trip of self-exploration and self-expression. But they also claim to have no idea where they're bound. They seem to think their minds are like loosely knit fishing nets that move through the water without catching any fish! They're proud possessors of the "Exoteric Wisdom" the young pilgrim John encountered in Lewis's first Christian publication, *The Pilgrim's Regress,* urging him to accept the fact that "wanting is better than having."[9] But endless discussion indicates lack of serious interest in truth, the quest for which becomes "an exciting game rather than a serious and exacting endeavor, a game in which, like the Caucus Race in 'Alice,' all are winners and receive the prize of official recognition."[10]

Few of today's students encounter honest teachers such as elderly chemist Bill Hingest, who (in *That Hideous Strength*) clung to a strong conviction concerning absolute truth. He warned a young sociologist, Mark, against getting involved with the National Institute of Coordinated Experiments (N.I.C.E.). Mark replied, "I suppose there are two views about everything."

Hingest responded, "Eh? Two views? There are a dozen views about everything until you know the answer. Then there's never more than one."[11]

During World War II, Lewis gave a series of lectures at the University of Durham, which were published as *The Abolition of Man*, probably Lewis's most profound ethical treatise, supporting virtuous living in accord with natural law.

His launching pad for the lectures was an elementary schoolbook he called "The Green Book." It overtly explained grammar but covertly taught that all values are subjective: truth is what we feel about things; all truth is subjective, and moral convictions are simply emotions.

Lewis urged his hearers to remember that Samuel Coleridge once overheard two tourists describe a waterfall. One thought it "sublime," inherently beautiful; the other declared it "pretty," personally pleasing. Lewis agreed with Coleridge, insisting there is something sublime *in* the waterfall itself.[12] If California's Yosemite Valley *is* sublime, Lewis would say, it has *inherent* beauty, something that makes it more beautiful than a small canyon near my townhouse in San Diego. Whether or not I even see Yosemite, it's really there. And it *is* beautiful, whether or not I ever see it. But if I see it, I respond right when I rejoice at its beauty. To the child who sees the grandeur of Yosemite Valley and says "I like Disneyland better," we wisely say, "You'll understand better someday!"

The outcome of this debate over objective truth, esoteric as it may seem to some, is the struggle that shapes our culture. Those who argue that everyone chooses his or her own values easily impose theirs on others. At first they simply want, as secular humanists, to place humanity atop the natural world, freely exploiting nature for their own advantage. Then they begin to manipulate others who are simply part of the natural world, the result of natural selection in the evolutionary process.

This stands out in thinkers, claiming to be postmodernists, who champion the philosophy of Friedrich Nietzsche. Enamored with their "will-to" power, they endeavor to move beyond good and evil, for they consider themselves, as Nietzsche declared, *Ubermenschen,* or supermen and superwomen.

Before the birth of postmodernism, Lewis anticipated one of its hallmarks, the "Poison of Subjectivism." He feared we would lose our ethical base, leading not only to "the 'abolition of man,' but to a reign of Nonsense, a deconstructed world of relativism, selfishness, and unbelief."[13]

Fulfilling Lewis's prediction, influential postmoderns such as Michael Foucault and Jacques Derrida deny the very existence of truth. Postmodernists dismiss the *objectivity* of truth, goodness, beauty—reducing everything to the products of the human mind—arguing that reality is a "social construction." Much like Milton's Satan, they think, "The mind is its own place, and in itself Can make a Heaven of Hell, a Hell of Heaven."

So "anything goes," and inevitably, "might makes right."

The plight of modernity, according to noted sociologist Pitrim Sorokin, is, "If a person has no strong convictions as to what is right and what is wrong, if he does not believe in any God or absolute moral values," if he disavows promises and lives simply for the pleasures of the moment, "what can guide and control his conduct toward other men? Nothing but his desires and lusts. Under these conditions he loses all rational and moral control, even plain common sense."[14]

Along with Sorokin, Lewis objected to this sensate culture. But besides protesting, he proposed a route out of the swamp of subjectivism. He championed the natural law, the central ethical tradition of Western civilization.

The Truth Demands a Natural Law

When he consented during World War II to give a series of lectures on the British Broadcasting Corporation (later published as *The Case for Christianity*), Lewis drew a bead on a secularizing society and focused the crosshair of his scope on "Right and Wrong as a Clue to the Meaning of the Universe."

Noting that people forever argue, Lewis observed that in the process they invoke a standard—like golfers citing intricate rules for the links—they all accept. Without some "natural law" to which all of us appeal, we could have no arguments. Why object to someone's behavior unless it's wrong?

To illustrate, one of Lewis's friends, Nevill Coghill, recorded Lewis's conversation with Rector Marett of Exeter College concerning a Viennese scientist, Voronoff, who had conducted an experiment designed to renew elderly men's sexual prowess by "splicing the glands of young apes" onto theirs.

"Remarkable, isn't it?" said Marett. Lewis replied that such a process would be "unnatural." Marett, a philosophy teacher, exclaimed, "Come, come! 'Unnatural'! What do you mean '*unnatural*'? Voronoff is part of Nature, isn't he? What happens in Nature must surely be natural. Speaking as a philosopher, don't you know, I can attach no meaning to your objection; I don't understand you!"

"I am sorry, Rector," Lewis replied, "but I think any philosopher from Aristotle to—say—Jeremy Bentham, would have understood me."

Undismayed, Marett waved off his philosophical predecessors as naive, declaring, "O well, we've got beyond Bentham by now, I hope. If Aristotle or he had known about Voronoff, they might have changed their ideas. Think of the possibilities he opens up! You'll be an old man yourself one day." Lewis wryly replied, *"I would rather be an old man than a young monkey."*[15]

To discover what is truly *natural*, Lewis guides us back to Aristotle's maxim: "To find out what is natural, we must study specimens which retain their nature and not those which have been corrupted."[16]

He also stressed that Edmund Spenser, one of his favorite medieval poets, understood nature "as Aristotle did—the 'nature' of anything being its unimpeded growth from within to perfection, neither checked by accident nor sophisticated by art. To this 'nature' his allegiance never falters."[17] Given to us along with human nature, the natural law, otherwise called "Traditional Morality or the First Principles of Practical Reason or the First Platitudes, is not one among a series of possible systems of value. It is the sole source of all value judgments."[18] In no way is this value system uniquely Christian, though some of its critics brand it as such to dismiss it. It is as ancient as the Code of Hammurabi, as indelible as the rainbow's spectrum. There's no more inventing ethics than decreasing gravity. Lewis believed if we have a natural law, we must also have a supernatural Lawgiver responsible for our moral standards.

We discern moral truth in the reality undergirding all that exists. Lewis generally shared the ancient-medieval view that *being* precedes *truth*, which discloses the *good*. "Goodness conforms the soul to reality itself," enabling it "to become disciplined, knowledgeable and, finally virtuous."[19]

So durable standards exist! "Unless the measuring rod is independent of the things measured, we can do no measuring."[20] We see this in many areas of life. "You call a man a bad golf player because you know what Bogey is. You call a boy's answer to a sum wrong because you know the right answer. You call a man cruel or idle because you have in mind a standard of kindness or diligence. And while you are making the accusation you have to accept the standard as a valid one. If you begin to doubt the standard you automatically doubt the cogency of your accusation."[21]

The success of his British Broadcasting Corporation lectures, which sought to awaken his hearers to the inner echoes of the natural law, led to a second series of radio talks, published as *Christian Behaviour*. In Lewis's judgment, major moralists such as Samuel Johnson always reminded people of what they tried to ignore. Some things you cannot not know: Great teachers bring us back to basic verities. Indeed, we can no more invent moral maxims than we can invent hydrogen and oxygen. We can no more conjure up standards like justice than we can make gold out of lead.

Like explorers discovering new lands, we find "laws" (principles by which things run) embedded in what's *real*. We don't impose or construct "laws" and then herd things into corrals of our own devising.

To Lewis, if there is no natural law, if legislators and judges, teachers and journalists, stitch together scraps of their own experiences and emotions, if we lose touch with objective truth, we'll be as lost as western pioneers without a map or a guide.

Despising the Truth—Seven Deadly Sins

In *Spenser's Images of Life*, C. S. Lewis devotes a chapter to "the image of evil" in the great poet's work. One category examined his "images of disease and defect," an examination of the seven deadly sins, for "every one of them is either diseased or deformed or both."[22] Given the constancy of human nature, we must deal with the same inner disease, the same shocking deformation, which comes from our sinful estate.

Lewis, however, routinely relied on the insights of medieval thinkers, with their delineation of seven deadly sins and seven saving virtues. He staunchly defended objective truths because he believed in the objective reality of God and of all that's eternal. Only what's eternal weighs in the ultimate scale of life, and eternal realities exist independently of us temporal creatures. So if we're wise, we'll look *outside* rather than *inside* ourselves. If we can know anything at all apart from our own feelings, there must be realities independent of us that we discover and know as they are, not as we choose to define them.

In the ancient world, early Christians wasted little time trying to persuade other people that they (other people) were sinners, for people generally recognized their plight. But times have changed. According to Lewis, Christians must first expose the evil, declare the bad news, before telling the good news of salvation. During the past century, Western thinkers have welded together a "humanitarian" creed, reducing goodness to "kindness," making sentimentality or compassion or benevolence (feelings rather than actions) the marks of righteousness.

Freud and his followers persuaded millions that neither God nor sin really exists. So, Lewis argued, we must deal honestly with sin. Jesus did! Unless we share His anger with, and sorrow for, humanity's sinfulness, we cannot grasp the import of His redemptive work for us.

If we face ourselves honestly, we feel guilt for sins committed. When we sin—slandering a spouse or stealing from a boss—we know it. We never admire it in others, and we know that God detests it. A God undisturbed by sin would not be God.

Living the Truth: The Seven Virtues

To live according to the natural law, many Christian ethicists have found the "virtue ethics" tradition most helpful. Rather than setting up a list of rules and trying to follow them, virtue ethics urge each of us to become a person of integrity, habitually doing what's right simply because it comes out of our inner being.

By encouraging his readers to cultivate the virtues, Lewis basically followed the established medieval Christian tradition that called for cultivating virtues. Moral rules enable us to live well, just as rules for athletic competitions enable games to take place. Morality entails fairness and equity between individuals, integrity and decency with individuals, and a common end toward which all people aim.

Though certain "rules" must be followed, the real reason for virtuous living is the role it plays in perfecting the person, helping him or her attain the end for which he or she was created. God wants healthy, holy people, Lewis maintained, not preprogrammed robots. He wants loyalty to Him as a person, not rigorous rule-tending.

Lewis's thought easily interfaces with the ethics of virtue evident in Aristotle and Aquinas and Hooker—recently reasserted by ethicists such as Alastair MacIntyre. Habits form us. Choices, like bricks laid in layers, build our character. Decade by decade, we become either "heavenly" or "hellish," growing closer to God or widening the chasm between us and Him.

The virtuous life, slowly shaping our character, enables us to respond to the challenges of this adventure called life.

Lewis explained that in Plato's *Republic,* youngsters were to be raised to see and admire what is good and beautiful so that choosing right would become second nature. Before we can reason, we must prepare to reason. Before we're adults, we must learn to act as adults. Virtues such as temperance and courage must be learned. So moral education, both in the schools and society, plays a large role in Lewis's thought. To rightly educate, Lewis proposed a medieval model portraying the rational soul as a fusion of two faculties: *intellectus* and *ratio*. With our *intellectus* we "just see" a "self-evident truth" such as the whole is greater than any one of its parts. With our *ratio* we move "step-by-step to prove a truth which is not self-evident."[23]

To take the right steps, to perfect our *ratio*, we need mentors, wise guides who show us through example and precept how to see and live in truth.

As he evaluated modern education, Lewis was not concerned by the lack of intellectual development, but by the "atrophy of the chest." Without this moral faculty, we may lament the loss of character and virtue, but we lack the means to develop these qualities.

What we need is *virtue*, moral strength and integrity, the true end of moral endeavors. In Plato's school, philosophers undergo a demanding, disciplined regimen. In basketball you must first master the arts of dribbling and passing, of shooting free throws and jump shots, before you can play in the games. Likewise, only as you mature as a virtuous person can you see the good and be good. Consequently, "for Plato the goal is nothing less than holiness, likeness to what is good."[24] And nothing less would satisfy C. S. Lewis.

PART ONE

THE SEVEN DEADLY SINS

1 ✎ Pride

"The Complete Anti-God State of Mind"

According to Christian teachers, the essential vice, the utmost evil, is Pride. . . . Pride leads to every other vice: it is the complete anti-God state of mind.[1]

IN HIS EARLY YEARS, C. S. Lewis wanted to be a poet. If modern poetry had not veered from traditional concerns for rhyme and meter, he might have made his mark as a (probably minor) English poet.

Though he focused his literary energies elsewhere, Lewis routinely wrote poems, one envisioning a young woman who desperately needs more wisdom:

> *I longed last night to make her know the truth*
> *That none of them has told her. Flushed with youth,*
> *Dazed with a half-hour triumph, she held the crowd.*
> *She loved the boys that buzzed on her like flies,*
> *She loved the envy in the women's eyes,*
> *Faster she talked. I longed to cry aloud,*
> *"What, has no brother told you yet, with whom,*
> *With what, you share the power that makes you proud?"*[2]

It's a bit like the little girl with a large cone of cotton candy who was asked, "How can a little girl like you eat all of that cotton candy?"

The little girl candidly responded, "Mister, I'm really much bigger on the inside than I am on the outside."[3]

Growing big on the inside shoves God to the outside. And that's where we find pride.

Pride Defined: Rejecting God and His Will

The most visible kind of pride, physical vanity, is actually one of its least lethal expressions. The most deadly form of pride has little to do with how a person looks. In its deepest sense, as Thomas Aquinas said, "Pride *[superbia]* is so called because a man thereby aims higher *[supra]* than he is."

Proud people seek to look better than they are. Thomas concluded, "He who wishes to overstep beyond what he is, is proud."[4]

Ultimately, "Pride has its beginning when a person abandons the Lord, his maker. Pride is like a fountain pouring out sin, and whoever persists in it will be full of wickedness."[5] Proud people want to soar like space shuttles, orbiting above God, preferring their own way to God's way. Pride is the sin that prompted Lucifer to abandon heaven and is the cardinal sin that cost Adam and Eve the bliss of Eden.

In one of his most profound statements, Lewis wrote, "There are only two kinds of people, in the end: those who say to God, 'Thy will be done' and those to whom God says, in the end, *'thy* will be done.'"[6]

The pride intent on having one's way permeates Lewis's *The Magician's Nephew*—chronologically the first of The Chronicles of Narnia—in which we learn how the land of Narnia was created. Young Digory (who later appears as the kindly old scholar who owns the house in *The Lion, the Witch, and the Wardrobe*) and his friend Polly are transported into another world through some magical rings crafted by Digory's evil Uncle Andrew. There they meet a beautiful witch, Queen Jadis, who tells them how an earlier world, the wondrous world of Charn, was destroyed. She and her sister had quarreled over who should rule the kingdom. Neither would give in. A war with magic ensued. Finally Jadis, losing the war, wielded the power of "the Deplorable Word" and annihilated everything but herself. All Charn's creatures—its people and animals—evaporated, as if in an atomic bomb attack. They were, she claimed, *hers,* so she could do anything she wanted with them. Only she survived, ruling a desolate, empty realm. But she was queen—"Queen of her World." She got her way!

Jadis claimed her sister was to blame for the destruction, for she had actually wanted to rule Charn. Projecting her own sin onto her sister, Jadis declared, "Her pride has destroyed the whole world."[7]

Of course, Jadis's own pride was what destroyed it. The evil queen personifies sin's deepest root: the "pride which would rather reign in hell than serve in heaven."[8] Lewis learned this truth, in part at least, from his spiritual mentor, George Macdonald, who said, "The one principle of hell is—'I am my own!'"[9]

When Digory questioned Jadis's destructive acts, she dismissed him as a "common boy" who could never fathom lofty political matters. She could do things he could not, for she was a *queen!* She need obey no mortal rules. She reminded Digory of his Uncle Andrew, who had once waved aside Digory's charge that it was "rotten" to break one of his promises. In response, Andrew said little boys should keep their word, but superior folks such as himself had a "hidden wisdom" that freed them from ordinary rules. "Ours," he said, using the same words as the witch, "is a high and lonely destiny."[10]

Falling captive to the serpent's words, Eve sought a similar "high and lonely destiny." Since then, her offspring have wrestled with the primordial sin of pride, the determination to shake off God's jurisdiction.

As in the ruins of ancient Charn, rendered barren by a witch's pride, so, too, throughout human history, earth's assorted ills underscore a moral darkness, a chasm of evil in the human heart. And it's all due to what Lewis discerned: at the heart of the human predicament is the root of all sins, pride.

As "the complete anti-God state of mind,"[11] pride is not as much *for* something as *against* something. Evil itself is not *something*—it's the *absence* of something. "Goodness is, so to speak, itself: badness is only spoiled goodness. And there must be something good first before it can be spoiled."[12]

"Evil is a parasite, not an original thing."[13] Thus, the source of all our ills comes from "putting yourself first—wanting to be the centre—wanting to be God."[14]

So while categorizing the infinite varieties of human waywardness into the "seven deadly sins," ancient and medieval theologians insisted, with Geoffrey Chaucer's Parson, that "the roote of all these sevene sinnes is Pryde, the general roote of all harmes."[15]

More than bragging or strutting, pride strikes a pose of independence from God, avoiding Him so as to slough off the strictures of His will. As Lewis understood, pride pits us against each other. Pride pits us, like stubborn two-year-olds defying their parents, against God. It's an onstage encore of our first parents' decision to "be as gods" or what Augustine called "the love of self in contempt of God."

Just as darkness excludes light, so sin excludes sanctity. Both sanctity and sin are states of *being* more than specific *acts*. While more dramatically displayed on the billboards of life in sinful deeds—rape, murder, theft, treason—sin as a *state of being* is the ultimate black hole of the spirit, the implosion of an inwardly gravitating self. This black hole is pride, and in his discussions of the pervasive power of evil and sin, Lewis continually reminds us to focus on it as the root of all sins.

When we are unwilling to trust God, we become proud. When we are overwhelmed with addictions of various sorts and still claim "I can handle it," we're proud. When "looking out for number one," we indulge our self-will and are proud. "This act of self-will on the part of the creature, which constitutes an utter falseness to its true creaturely position, is the only sin that can be conceived as the Fall."[16]

Refusing to trust God's providential and loving power, we seek a tainted and twisted power—a Promethean power—for ourselves. And we especially crave power *over* others—to *rule* the family, the school, the church, the nation. "Inordinately enamored of its own power," Augustine said, pride "despises the more just dominion of a higher authority."[17]

To become a Christian means submitting to the Father! We surrender our will to His will. It means crucifying self-will, self-seeking, self-sovereignty. To surrender to our husband, or to our supervisor at work, or to our mother or father is a small step in breaking the pride that separates us from God.

Skilled horse trainers "break" a wild mustang through a series of small steps—putting on the bridle, then the saddle, leading the horse, then putting some weight in the saddle—before actually riding it. Likewise, God "breaks" our pride in order to transform us into His own.

Spiritual Pride—The Most Damning of All

One of the ghosts in *The Great Divorce* (a beguiling story in which Lewis wonders what might happen if a group from hell took an excursion to the boundary of heaven and had the opportunity to change quarters) illustrates pride's deepest problem: self-righteousness. Recalling his earthly life, the ghost claimed to have lived a decent life. Not that he was religious or perfect, but he'd tried hard to be good. And, he noted, he never demanded anything but his "rights."[18]

When we pretend we've always done our best, when we don't want anything that's not due us, then we abolish any need for God's grace, any need for the salvation that comes to us as a gift from above.

Pride's most insidious form is spiritual pride, shrewdly counterfeiting holiness. Pretentious humility is pride at its worst.

The most depraved people are those who pretend to be perfect, to rival the holiness of God! When we feel religiously superior to others, the devil's at our side. But when we are aware of God, we forget about ourselves, unable to even imagine ourselves superior to anyone!

So the demonic Screwtape instructs Wormwood to tempt his subject, who has become an enthusiastic Christian, to embrace "the strongest and most beautiful of the vices—Spiritual Pride."[19] To get the young convert to so embrace all things Christian, to devote himself unreservedly to the Cause, might open a trapdoor through which he could be sucked to destruction. To be appropriately "different" from wordly folks, to delight in being part of a select "set" of spiritual folks, sets one up for Satan's seductions. Anything to get a person to feel part of the "inner ring," a select circle, an elite corps—especially of "spiritual" folks!

"Inner Ring" Group Pride

Ultimately, pride blinds us. We never really "win" when standing atop others, and our pretenses cannot endure scrutiny, for as Lewis says, "No man who says *I'm as good as you* believes it. He would not say it if he did. The St. Bernard never says it to the toy dog, nor the scholar to the dunce, nor the employable to the bum, nor the pretty woman to the plain."[20] Yet in one of the

ironies of history, the foulest sin condemned by medieval theologians has been acclaimed and enthroned as a positive virtue
by modern "humanists." Autonomous individualism, the fertile
soil for the "human rights" crusades so frequently invoked by
secular thinkers, is little more than rationalized pride.

Such pride infects individuals, of course, but it also affects
groups, which are especially prone to dominate others. Especially dangerous is the desire to join the "inner ring" of various
groups. Indeed, this desire to join the "inner ring" plays an important place in Lewis's understanding of sin. The paper wherein he referred to himself as a "middle-aged moralist" was titled
"The Inner Ring," a probing analysis of the "World" and its
ways. In every group of people, he says, there are two hierar-
chies: the obvious one of ranks and position and the hidden
one constituted by those who are insiders. The Inner Ring has
its unique ways of speaking, knowing glances, caustic snobbery.
While magnetically alluring, inner rings subtly pervert persons
who enter them. "Of all passions the passion for the Inner Ring
is most skillful in making a man who is not yet a very bad man
do very bad things."[21]

To join the president's cabinet, a denomination's general
board, or a college's faculty council easily leads to a prideful
sense of superiority by virtue of position. Even self-help groups
and human rights lobbying endeavors, seeking to "empower"
their members, easily slide into pride, shading the truth and
crushing their enemies to secure their goals. Far more evil than a
woman taking "pride" in her appearance is the pride of "world-
changers" intent on imposing their vision of how the world
should be. Contemporary philosopher Peter Kreeft, who celebrates Lewis's insights, notes that "the exemplars of pride are
not movie stars but dictators. Movie stars are vain; dictators are
proud."[22] Dictators—and demagogic democratic politicians—obviously want power.

The personification of such pride resides in one of Lewis's fictional characters, Weston, a brilliant physicist who seeks (in both
Out of the Silent Planet and *Perelandra*) to bring other planets under his control. All his endeavors, he asserted, were devoted to
perpetuating the human race in space. He was, hand-in-glove
with many utopian social planners, overtly "unselfish" in his

plans and utterly ruthless in carrying them out. In a revealing monologue in *Perelandra*, in which he tried to entrap the "Green Lady" and precipitate another Evelike planetary fall, Weston called Ransom (his righteous adversary) an "Idiot" for espousing traditional values. He equated his own pantheistic thoughts with those of the universe, and he believed himself to be the cusp of a creatively evolving cosmos. Incredibly, he said, "I am it. Do you see, you timid, scruple-mongering fool? I *am* the Universe. I, Weston, am your God and your Devil."[23]

Utopian Arrogance: Engineering a World

In a very real sense, many "moderns" like Weston celebrate pride's reign. Powerful people dot the covers of *Vogue* and *People* and *Business Week* magazines. Hollywood elites revel in their celebrity status, which enables them to exert political power. World-shakers and crowd-pleasers stand atop our social pyramids. As a result of currents unleashed by the Renaissance and Enlightenment, Peter Kreeft says, "Our civilization has been redirecting more and more of its spiritual interest and energy away from the traditional goal of conforming the soul to God and to the new goal of conforming the world to the desires of the soul."[24]

In part, C. S. Lewis wrote space fictions such as *Perelandra* to counteract—or at least warn against—power-based ideologies such as Marxism, humanism, and feminism. Such *isms* still pulsate like radio signals throughout the modern world. He explained that "Westonism" refers to the passionate faith some folks place in progress, the hope "of perpetuating and improving the human race" and of overcoming death itself.[25] Westonism has flourished like bindweed for two centuries, seeking to establish "the heavenly city of the eighteenth century *philosophes*"[26] in Enlightenment-shaped circles. Lewis's first "Christian" book, *The Pilgrim's Regress,* features "John" on a journey away from his birthplace, "Puritania," an old-fashioned land ruled by the "Landlord" who prescribed the rules for his tenants. One of the first persons young John encountered was "Mr. Enlightenment," who dismissed those who believed in a "Landlord." He did this simply because of "Christopher Columbus, Galileo, the earth [being] round, [the] invention of printing, gunpowder!!"[27] Such non sequitors meant nothing more than air leaking from a punctured tire, but Mr. Enlightenment lacked rigorous training in logic. He simply assumed that modern "scientific" theories, making humanity potentially omniscient, had forever discredited Christianity.

That assumption clearly nurtured the evil men who sought to establish a utopian society through N.I.C.E. in Lewis's third space fiction, *That Hideous Strength*. When Lord Feverstone recruited Mark to work for the institute, he declared that men of science had finally gained power to control everything. Mark, he said, could join that future-shaping corps of enlightened scientists. "'Man has got to take charge of Man,' Feverstone said."[28] He and Mark could join the elite pioneers who would make "a new type of man."[29]

Those enamored with creating "a new type of man" in our century generally fly various designs of the "socialist" flag—one of Christianity's most deadly adversaries. A century ago, Fyodor Dostoyevsky, speaking through the character Alyosha, said if "God and immortality did not exist he would at once have become an atheist and a socialist. For socialism is not merely the labor question, it is before all things the atheistic question, the question of the form taken by atheism today, the question of the tower of Babel built without God, not to mount to Heaven from earth but to set up Heaven on earth."[30]

Long before the "successes" of socialist revolutions in Russia and China, Dostoyevsky discerned the underlying currents constituting socialist ideology: the denial of God and His authority in our world.

Lewis deeply distrusted all such utopian schemes, as did Nobel Prize winning economist Friedrich A. von Hayek, who elaborated, Edwin A. Feulner says, "a simple yet profound truth: man does not and cannot know everything, and when he acts as if he does, disaster follows."[31] Feulner explains:

> Hayek's stunningly simple insight was that the biblical warning, "pride goeth before a fall," applies to societies as well as individuals, and that hubris is a tragic flaw not only for ancient Greek heroes, but also for modern nation states. He recognized that socialism, the collectivist state, and planned economies represent the ultimate form of hubris, for those who plan them attempt—with insufficient knowledge—to redesign the nature of man. In so doing they arro-

gantly disregard traditions that embody the wisdom of generations; impetuously disregard customs whose purpose they do not understand; and blithely confuse the law written on the hearts of men—that they cannot change—with administrative rules that they can alter at whim. For Hayek, such presumption was not only "fatal conceit," but also "the road to serfdom"—the title of his famous denunciation of socialism, published in 1944.[32]

Scripture summarizes, "Pride goes before destruction, and a haughty spirit before a fall" (Prov. 16:18, NKJV).

2 ✑ Envy

"The Most Odious of Vices"

*Envy always brings the truest charge,
or the charge nearest to the truth,
that she can think up; it hurts more.*[1]

THE YEAR BEFORE HE DIED, C. S. Lewis wrote a preface to a new edition of *The Screwtape Letters*, noting that evil occurs not only in the criminal conspiracies or "concentration camps and labour camps" but, more malevolently, "in clean, carpeted, warmed, and well-lighted offices, by quiet men with white collars and cut fingernails and smooth-shaven cheeks who do not need to raise their voice. Hence, naturally enough, my symbol for Hell is something like the bureaucracy of a police state or the offices of a thoroughly nasty business concern."[2]

A competitive "survival of the fittest" environment, a "dog eat dog" behavior reigns in hell, Lewis thought. And it has many earthly outposts. "Everyone wishes everyone else's discrediting, demotion, and ruin; everyone is an expert in the confidential report, the pretended alliance, the stab in the back."[3]

Sorrow at Another's Good

Envy sorrows at another's good. It rears its head like an aroused rattlesnake when someone else enjoys success. It prompts us, when we fail, to pity ourselves and pout. Disgruntled, we sulk when others succeed, aping the Grinch, one of Dr. Seuss's characters, who bites himself whenever someone else enjoys something.

In time, envy, like a burning coal, consumes itself. In the

words of John Chrysostom, "As a moth gnaws at a garment, so envy consumes a man." This truth surfaces in an ancient Jewish story that tells of an angel visiting a storekeeper and offering to give him whatever he wished—knowing that his main rival would get twice as much. Perversely, the man asked to be blinded in one eye.

Such is the nature of envy—harm your rivals, no matter what it costs you. As Helmut Schoeck insists, "the envious man" may not even "want to have the coveted asset, nor could he enjoy it," but he can't stand someone else having it. "He becomes ill with annoyance over someone else's private yacht although he has never wished to board a ship in his life."[4] Unlike simple jealousy, which hungers to possess others' talents or possessions or relationships—such as a mother's attention or a husband's affection—envy simply dislikes the fact that someone else has something, be it a Mercedes, an honorary title, a job or accolade, a dress, or a newspaper headline.

Ever a Deadly Sin

In envy, Thomas Aquinas says, "We grieve over a man's good, in so far as his good surpasses ours; this is envy properly speaking, and is always sinful."[5] To want a coat or a comfortable house or a reliable car, such as others possess, is not necessarily envy. Nor is it wrong to want to get ahead in your job as others have, receiving the honor and salary of a higher position. Desiring what's good is good! Paul even said, "If any one aspires to the office of bishop, he desires a noble task" (1 Tim. 3:1, RSV).

On the other hand, one encrusted with envy sees a bishop or another person doing well in his or her career, and hopes to pull that person down, hoping his or her demotion might result in the envious one's own promotion. Envy, like a basketball player jostling others aside to get a rebound, seeks their disadvantage.

Consequently, envy roots itself in pride and flowers in hate. Envy's essence is graphically captured in the German word *schadenfreude*, which means "malicious joy." *Schadenfreude* is the "worst trait in human nature," declared philosopher Arthur Schopenhauer. He discerned how its venom infected both those who praise bad folks (making a celebrity out of someone who has committed bad deeds) and those who withhold praise for those who do something good, fearing any praise for others keeps that person from receiving praise.[6]

In *The Last Battle*, the sixth of Lewis's Narnian Chronicles, a small band of good, loyal creatures join King Tirian and the lordly lion Aslan to battle the evil followers of the Ape, who schemes to rule Narnia. On the sidelines stand sullen dwarfs who support neither the Ape nor Aslan. They trust neither the Antichrist nor the Christ. They lose, so choosing, everlasting life, because they want to make Narnia a place for themselves, serving neither their rightful king (Tirian) nor the newly victorious Calormene invaders, who support the Ape.

At a critical point in the story, Aslan called the dwarfs to join him, but they urged each other to discount his invitation, to deny his truth. Persevering in his call, Aslan, like Jesus feeding the 5,000, miraculously made a banquet for them—exotic foods and good wine. They ate, but they gulped and swallowed without so much as tasting it. Soon they looked around and suspected other dwarfs had more or better food. They tried to grab more from those nearby, and they assailed each other and failed to follow Aslan.[7]

Dwarflike, jaundice-eyed envy secures its own position by shredding others. It's the flipside, the constant bedfellow, of pride. Strangely enough, envy walks hand-in-hand with feelings of both superiority and inferiority. The proud person thinks he or she is superior to others, lording it over all rivals. The one feeling inferior, on the other hand, pities himself or herself and tries to level inequities, often pointing out others' failures to reduce their standing.

Unlike those guilty of pride, however, few folks honestly confess to envy. It's a vice that does not elicit the standing ovations given to entertainers or the glossy magazine pages dedicated to models. Parents don't seek to inculcate it in children or admire it in themselves. Yet it clearly permeates everything. We feel envy in ourselves, we see it in others, and we usually share the medieval view that envy is one of the seven deadly sins, agreeing with Chaucer's Parson, who called it a "foul sin," perhaps "the worst sin there is," for it is "against all virtues and goodnesses."[8]

This perspective was clarified in the fourth century by Basil of Caesarea, who said, "No vice more pernicious than envy is implanted in the souls of men." An envious person never knows joy, for he or she inevitably sees prosperous, happy homes, things that cut his or her heart like a sword and "aggravate the sickness and add to the pain of the envious." Envy is an attitude that can't be divulged, while its host must secretly secrete his or her bile and store it in the cesspool of the soul, a "disease which is gnawing at his [or her] vitals and consuming them." Still more, Basil says, "Envy is the most savage form of hatred."

Envying, we want less for others. Envying, we resent others' good fortune, pleased when they suffer loss and pain, elated when they fall from grace or fail in their endeavors. Since nothing is positive or self-affirming in it, we harm ourselves as we envy. The irony of envy is that in shooting at others we usually shoot at ourselves.

Social Envy—Egalitarianism

In the past, moralists focused on personal envy, which seems forever present in humanity's heart. During the past 200 years, however, the vice has assumed a more social stance, stemming from modernity's fascination with "equality." French revolutionaries, who demanded "liberty, equality, fraternity," celebrated envy's prospects and helped birth the revolutions that have shaped the modern world. So to many, equality is self-evidently good. To some it is the greatest of all goods. As a result, Hannah Arendt, one of this century's finest thinkers, pointed out,

> Modern man has come to resent everything given, even his own existence—to resent the very fact that he is not the creator of the universe and himself. In this fundamental resentment, he refuses to see rhyme or reason in the given world. In his resentment of all laws merely given to him, he proclaims openly that everything is permitted and believes secretly that everything is possible.[9]

C. S. Lewis, often at odds with the "modern world," countered, "When equality is treated not as a medicine or a safety-gadget but as an ideal, we begin to breed that stunted and envious sort of mind which hates all superiority."[10]

We find disproportionate numbers of influential anthropologists and sociologists—personified by the sociologist Mark in Lewis's novel *That Hideous Strength*—committed to an egalitarian and utopian ideal. Thus, they have disguised envy with socially accepted and academically crafted masks—compassion for the oppressed, support for the "marginalized," identification with the poor. All social problems, such theorists imagine, would disappear "in a society of absolute equals." So utopias, such as the one envisioned by N.I.C.E. in Lewis's story, are proposed and laws are passed to build them.

Such a society, of course, never has nor ever could exist. The "Golden Age" of primitive tribesmen living without envy and in egalitarian bliss can be found only in the pages of books. Yet thinkers from Rousseau to Marx have urged us to construct their imagined worlds. Unable to adjust to the real world, they want to remake it to fit their designs.

Lewis, on the contrary, placed his "perfect" world in outer space on the planet Malacandra, where, in *Out of the Silent Planet*, we find creatures perfectly willing to obey their Creator. Unlike the utopias made by humanity, heavens on earth resulting from human engineering, Lewis knew that only in God's heaven, where all persons' sinful natures have been finally transformed by grace, could we live as we're designed to live.

As Lewis noted, we should never indulge in envy simply because it's expressed by a group instead of an individual. To wish to bring down a certain group, such as the "Capitalists" or "White Men" or "Heterophobes," is as evil as for us to wish our boss would lose his or her position.

Certainly we're equals before God, and in a democracy all citizens entering the polling booth can claim equality. But in few other realms should we do so. As Lewis insisted, "Human nature will not permanently endure flat equality if it is extended from its proper political field into the more real, more concrete fields within. Let us *wear* equality; but let us undress every night."[11]

A Democratic Dilemma

Lewis, like many who study history, reflected on the pervasive influence of envy in democratic circles. On a political level, democracy seems to be a viable system of government; it may well be most appropriate for the 20th century. Yet it encourages a spurious notion of "equality" that awakened Lewis's ire. Long before various self-interest groups cried for their "rights," Lewis warned that societies that encourage people to think everyone is equal disintegrate into squabbling factions.

In "Screwtape Proposes a Toast," a section Lewis later appended to his classic *The Screwtape Letters,* Screwtape tells us that egalitarian claims, apart from civil rights, are typically "made only by those who feel themselves to be in some way inferior." Their innards churn with an "itching, smarting, writhing awareness of an inferiority which the patient refuses to accept." What they cannot accept they resent.

> **Now, this useful phenomenon is in itself by no means new. Under the name of Envy it has been known to the humans for thousands of years. But hitherto they always regarded it as the most odious, and also the most comical, of vices. . . . The delightful novelty of the present situation is that you can sanction it—make it respectable and even laudable—by the incantatory use of the word** *democratic.*[12]

So we find examples of envy in democratic societies that adopt the progressive income and inheritance taxes—both, incidentally, planks in *The Communist Manifesto*'s proposal for social transformation. Helmut Schoeck insists there is an insidious "appeal of envy in politics" that promises "an unattainable equality" by taking from the rich and giving to the poor. "Rob Peter to pay Paul" is an ancient refrain.

Demagogic politicians shrewdly make rich people feel guilty for prospering, for rising above others. To alleviate their guilt, without giving away their own fortunes, the rich propose taxes designed to rectify social injustices. So we find the familiar story of well-to-do politicians proposing more social programs, ignoring the evidence that similar programs have failed.

Such rhetoric, for politicians and wealthy people who refuse to confess and repent of their own sins, proves therapeutic, relieving their inner sense of guilt. Since by nature people want more power and money, any move by the state to play Robin Hood will gain popular acclaim.

Consequently, within the past century, we've witnessed the replacement of government as watchman to government as social worker. Unfortunately, once started, the process of government satisfying people's desires will not end, as we witness in the events of the French Revolution, in which the lands of the aristocrats and church properties were confiscated without satisfying the populace's hunger.

Envy has little bearing on real needs, only comparative positions. So everyone compares his or her slot in society with those who have more and hungers to erase all inequalities. Since these hungers cannot be satiated, special interest groups proliferate for more entitlements.

In one area that concerned him deeply, C. S. Lewis feared the impact of a democratic egalitarianism that seeks "to propitiate evil passions, to appease envy" by eliminating standards in schools and treating all students alike. Since intelligence and ability will always place some students above others, no leveling endeavors can effectively eliminate them.[13]

What Lewis feared in the 1940s has become standard policy today. Schools major in self-esteem. Churches encourage self-development, promoting "growth groups" and therapy sessions in which no one confesses sin but targets someone else for causing him or her grief.

And popular psychologists amplify the message. Walt Whitman declared, "The whole theory of the universe is directed unerringly to one single individual—namely to You." This quotation graced the frontispiece of Wayne Dyer's *Your Erroneous Zones,* one of the best-selling books of the therapeutic culture. If you are the most important person in the world, certainly you're entitled to a vast or infinite storehouse of pleasures and privileges. When frustrations ensue, obviously someone else is responsible for your pain—and you're free to whine about your misfortunes!

Radical Feminism

Almost always the whiner vents anger about inequities of some sort. Envy erupts in anger at perceived injustices. Envy interprets differences as unfair, human-devised inequalities. Radical feminism that seeks, as Christina Hoff Sommers shows,[14] to overhaul human nature illustrates such envy. For example, claiming to speak for fellow feminists, Shulamith Firestone tells us that the life of America's suburban housewives resembles that of Nazi Holocaust victims because living in a patriarchal society suffocates women. To gain true equality, she thinks, women must be treated the same as men. Firestone asserts that feminists must "question not just all of Western culture, but the organization of culture itself, and further *even the very organization of nature.*"[15]

Such thinking, Joyce Little comments, imagines that "Reality . . . begins in the human mind and then proceeds to change the outer or material world, beginning with the human body itself. All of reality is shaped by the human mind."[16]

To C. S. Lewis, sexual self-pity and its animosity are skillfully applied to cover envy and major in denying reality. Such thinking, he warned, results from the "poison of subjectivism," imagining we can make the world conform to our wishes. He feared that radical feminist ideology, since it denies the reality of sexual differences, would violate the Creator's plan and disrupt normal roles of men and women in marriage.

Our *nature* as male and female assigns us different *roles* in creation. "Have as much equality as you please—the more the better—in our marriage laws: but at some level," Lewis insisted, "consent to inequality, nay, delight in inequality, is an *erotic* necessity."[17] Both men and women find everlasting joy in celebrating the other's difference—the unique feminine and masculine traits that bring balance to a union—and delight in giving the other attitudes utterly opposite to envy and its incessant competition.

The development of one of Lewis's most alluring fictional characters, Jane, in *That Hideous Strength,* illuminates one of his deepest convictions. As the book begins, Jane is discontented with Mark, her professionally ambitious husband, and with the state of marriage. Yet something about the words of her wedding vows haunted her. Perhaps marriage held something, a deeper level of reality, that she had not yet experienced. Perhaps her vows, celebrating the sacramental depths of a covenant, if implemented, would satisfy the deep hungers of her heart. Events in the story led her to realize that submitting to God, which included submitting to her husband, provided the ultimate key to the good life she desired.

More than propounding a theory, Lewis himself found joy only as he submitted to God's will for his life. Like a woman surrendering to her man, or a medieval lady surrendering to her knightly lord, Lewis surrendered to the Lord of all and found in Him the joy he sought.

In truth, young women who insist on equality, says Danielle Crittenden, easily "waste the opportunity in our passionate young to find lasting love and everything that goes with it—home, children, stability, and the pleasure of sex as an expression of profound, romantic, and monogamous love. . . . We might now be more free. But we enjoy less happiness, less fulfillment, less dignity, and, of all things, less romance."[18]

How strange it is, she says, that modern North America values "the work a woman does writing legal briefs more than the hours she might have devoted to helping her child feel her importance in the world."[19] The world can do without more lawyers. What it needs is better—and more highly valued—mothers.

Mothers and fathers, parents and children, teachers and students, statesmen and subjects—all have righteous roles to play in a good world. To accept one's position, to love and laud those in other positions, even when they are "above" us, marks a righteous person, for "a sound heart is the life of the flesh: but envy the rottenness of the bones" (Prov. 14:30, KJV).

3 ✎ Anger

"The Anesthetic of the Mind"

Anger's the anesthetic of the mind.[1]

In 1894 the Baltimore Orioles played a game with their rivals in Boston. The Orioles' legendary John McGraw provoked a fight with the rival team's third baseman, which soon erupted into a full-fledged brawl on the field. Fans jumped into the fight. Someone set fire to the stands, and the entire park burned to the ground. The fire then spread to nearby buildings, and 107 buildings in Boston burned—all because two baseball players vented their anger!

Driving America's freeways and walking its streets, we often see raised fists, vulgar gestures, challenges to fight. Words fly with the velocity and sharpness of spears. Voices inch up the decibel scale, sweeping aside reason and reconciliation. Taunts too often move us to violent acts. Raw anger bubbles like lava underlying the crust of many social interactions.

In Solomon Schimmel's judgment, "Anger plays a central role in assault, child abuse, murder and many rapes, and in interethnic and international violent conflict. Of the seven deadly sins, anger is the most pervasive, injurious to self and others, and most responsible for unhappiness and psychopathological behavior."[2]

Yet the word and the emotion it describes need clarification. Unlike some "deadly sins," such as lust or covetousness, anger has a good and evil side. We must differentiate between "righteous anger" and "sinful anger." For all its destructiveness, anger

43

at its deepest level is simply a natural emotion, understandable as a springlike reaction that snaps back against those who harm us. C. S. Lewis wrote, "Anger is the fluid that love bleeds when you cut it."[3] And like all emotions, our issue is how we deal with anger, how we channel it for good or evil.

The Good Anger

Righteous anger marks a holy man or woman. The Greek language has two words for anger. *Thumos* describes the rapid, explosive emotion that responds to injury or injustice. When someone sticks a knife in your back, you bleed. That's a normal, healthy reaction to the injury. When someone attacks us or an innocent person, we feel anger. It's a normal, healthy reaction to assault or danger.

In one Narnian adventure, the Lord Drinian (commanding *The Dawn Treader,* which is on its way to the end of the world), erupted when the mouse, Reepicheep, jumped overboard in his zeal to experience the new waters the ship had entered.

> **"Drat that mouse!" said Drinian. . . . "If there is any scrape to be got into, in it will get! It ought to be put in irons—keelhauled—marooned—have its whiskers cut off." . . .**
>
> **All this didn't mean that Drinian really disliked Reepicheep. On the contrary he liked him very much and was therefore frightened about him, and being frightened put him in a bad temper—just as your mother is much angrier with you for running out into the road in front of a car than a stranger would be.[4]**

Drinian resembles the generally admirable "Sanguine" man Lewis discusses in *The Discarded Image.* Such a man's "anger is easily roused but short-lived, he is a trifle peppery, but not sullen or vindictive."[5] So, as Aristotle argued, "A person is praised who is angry for the right reasons, with the right people, and also in the right way, at the right time and for the right length of time. . . . It is a slavish nature that will submit to be insulted or let a friend be insulted unresistingly."[6]

We certainly can "be . . . angry, and sin not" (Eph. 4:26, KJV), as Scripture says. Thomas Aquinas argued someone who "is angry with cause shall not" endanger his soul, "for without anger, teaching will be useless, judgments unstable, crimes unchecked."[7] So "if one is angry according to right reason, then to get angry is praiseworthy."[8]

As one would expect, Lewis shared this classical and Christian perspective. In the second volume of his space trilogy, *Perelandra*, Lewis portrays his hero, Elwin Ransom, valiantly battling the devilish physicist Weston. They ultimately engage in a hand-to-hand physical combat, which culminates with Weston's death. As the struggle began, Ransom felt what "perhaps no good man can ever have in our world . . . a torrent of perfectly unmixed and lawful hatred" that was fiercely determined to destroy evil. Amazingly, "this filled Ransom not with horror but with a kind of joy. The joy came from finding at last what hatred was made for."[9]

When anger leads one to defend the powerless, to disarm the aggressor, to avenge injustice, it shows "what hatred was made for" and displays its good side. In *The Last Battle,* Narnia's King Tirian responded vigorously to a Dryad's report that the talking trees were being felled by invading Calormenes in a place called Lantern Waste. "'Murdering the talking trees?' cried the King leaping to his feet and drawing his sword. 'How dare they?'"[10]

When the Dryad (a spirit of a tree) fell dead and vanished, Tirian ached with an anger no words could express. He resolved to act against the aggressors and strode toward the valley where the trees were falling. Fording a river, his wrath even insulated him from the chill of the water.

At various times in *The Chronicles of Narnia*, when Aslan's followers wage war for their Lord, they express a righteous anger. For there is indeed a strength, a holy outrage at evil and injustice, which impels people to take up arms and fight for what's right. Such "righteous anger" fuels holy causes, inspires holy acts.

This anger prompted some moms to form Mothers Against Drunk Driving to sensitize the public to the evils caused by drinking and driving. One can "be . . . angry, and sin not" when one's singularly angry with sin, not those who sin.

Martin Luther noted, "When I am angry I can write, pray, and preach well, for then my whole temperament is quickened, and my understanding sharpened, and all mundane vexations and temptations depart."[11] Thus, Lewis, speaking through characters such as the Dimbles in his space fictions, and through the lion, Aslan, in his Narnian chronicles, reveals that good anger gives one the courage to stand up for what's right.

However, real warriors—those who battle for the Lord—do so without rancor or hate. Their anger is almost dispassionate. It's an obviously objective stance, selfless—even self-sacrificing—rather than self-expressive.

The Evil Anger

Though our anger can be healthy at times, it's generally self-serving and rarely righteous. Too few of us become angry when others are mistreated. We may bemoan their plight but do little to help. Yet we routinely erupt with anger when we feel we are treated unfairly by others. The Greek language identifies the evil kind of anger as *orge,* which means a lasting, furious, vengeful desire to see an enemy suffer.

Though the phrase "without a cause" (which is added to "angry" in Matt. 5:22, KJV) is not found in the best Greek manuscripts, both John Chrysostom and Augustine, who preached at the end of the fourth century, relied on versions that included the clause. They felt the anger Jesus condemned needed to be clearly understood as a will to vengeance rather than an emotional reaction. This anger is maliciously setting the will, *harboring* resentment, *nursing* a grudge.

Such uncontrolled anger—and most anger is out of control—devours both its hosts and objects. Sinful anger gets upset at imagined insults and vents anathemas at all who differ from its host. Yet with consummate skill we generally disguise this sin by flying the flag of "justice," for as Thomas Aquinas says, "The angry man desires another's evil under the aspect of just revenge."[12]

The problem with evil anger is the inner attitude, the hate that desires to harm others. It's the desire for revenge, to do harm, to kill. As George Macdonald wrote, "It may be infinitely less evil to murder a man than to refuse to forgive him. The former may be the act of a moment of passion: the latter is the heart's choice. It is spiritual murder, the worst, to hate, to brood over the feeling that excludes, that, in our microcosm, kills the image, the idea of the hated."[13]

In *The Great Divorce*, we encounter one of Lewis's characters, Len, who (on earth) had killed a man named Jack. Both Len and Jack were now "solid" people, saved by God's Grace. In the story, Len meets one of the ghosts, his former boss, who was on the excursion from hell that forms the book's structure. The boss couldn't comprehend how a murderer gained entrance to heaven. Len explained that killing his coworker in a fit of rage wasn't as evil as the hatred he harbored, for years, against his boss. In his heart he'd wanted to kill him. Awake at night, like a coach envisioning plays for his team, he'd plotted the murder he'd never enacted. For that, he confessed, "I was the worst."[14]

The authority for Lewis's view is Jesus, who internalized the Old Testament's prohibition of murder: "You have heard that it was said to the people long ago, 'Do not murder, and anyone who murders will be subject to judgment.' But I tell you that anyone who is angry with his brother will be subject to judgment" (Matt. 5:21-22).

Rightly rooted in Jesus' teaching, Christian thinkers have identified anger as one of the sins that surely separate us from God. Much like Jesus' brother, James, they counsel, "Wherefore, my beloved brethren, let every man be swift to hear, slow to speak, slow to wrath: For the wrath of man worketh not the righteousness of God" (James 1:19-20, KJV).

Another form of cold, burning anger dominated and slowly devoured one of Lewis's finest fictional characters, Orual, the Queen of Glome in *Till We Have Faces*, the novel he judged as his best work. She had persuaded herself that powerful love for her sister, Psyche, was actually a form of jealousy—a possessiveness that sustained a subtle hatred. Orual needed to be needed—that was her notion of love. Such selfish "love" actually hates its beloved.

So when Psyche chose union with a god in a self-giving sacrifice, Orual allowed her bitterness to wither her soul. Her teacher, the Greek slave Fox, wisely responded to one of her outbursts, "Daughter, daughter. You are transported beyond all reason and nature. Do you know what it is? There's one part love in your heart, and five parts anger, and seven parts pride."[15]

Orual also imagined that she loved the brave soldier Bardia, who taught her to fight in strategic battles. But she resented the time he spent at home with his wife; she resented the fact that he once declared that his service for the queen was his daily work and less important to him than his time with his wife. When Bardia died, worn out by the demands she made upon him, Orual visited his widow, Ansit, who rebuked the queen for her insensitivity. "The mines," she said, "are not the only place where a man can be worked to death."[16]

She continued, comparing the sexes, saying that men are "harder, but we're tougher. They do not live longer than we. They do not weather a sickness better. Men are brittle."[17] Ansit knew that Queen Orual, inwardly seething at Bardia's devotion to his wife, had shattered him.

Facing this truth, the queen felt a "flash of anger [passing] through me, then a horror of misgiving."[18] She denied Ansit's accusation. But, after more conversation, she had to deal honestly with the love she had felt for Bardia. It was like the possessive love she had had for her sister. At long last, "those divine Surgeons had me tied down and were at work. My anger protected me only for a short time; anger wearies itself out and truth comes in. For it was all true—truer than Ansit could know."[19]

Malevolent anger, *orge,* is succinctly phrased in the motto some people proclaim: "Don't get angry—get even."

But it is difficult, if not impossible, to "get even." We usually harm ourselves more than our enemies when we try to right the scales of justice. Consider the case of a woman who came to Ibn Saud, the first king of Saudi Arabia, in 1932. She asked the king to execute the man who had killed her husband. The accused man had been gathering dates in a palm tree, slipped, and fell on her husband, fatally injuring him.

The king asked if the fall had been deliberate, or if the two men were enemies. Apparently they didn't know each other, and the fall was accidental. But the widow demanded revenge: life for life.

Ibn Saud tried to reason with her, urging her to accept a cash settlement or something else. But she insisted. Finally the king said, "It is your right to exact compensation, and it is also your right to ask for this man's life. But it is my right to decree how he shall die. You shall take this man with you, and he shall be tied to the foot of a palm tree, and then you yourself shall climb to the top of the tree and cast yourself down upon him from that height. In that way you will take his life as he took your husband's." There was a long pause. "Or perhaps," Ibn Saud added, "you would prefer after all to take the blood money?" The widow took the money.[20]

The bitterness that almost devoured Orual did damn a woman in Lewis's *The Great Divorce*. Her son Michael had died, and for 10 years she had nursed her grief, ignoring all else to hoard her memory of lost designs for him. Given the opportunity to actually join him in heaven, however, she had no interest unless she could once again be in control of her beloved Michael. She demanded he be returned to her. Heaven's ways were not her ways! So she rejected heaven! "I don't believe in a God who keeps mother and son apart," she moaned. "I believe in a God of Love."[21] Unless she could *possess* her boy, she had no interest in his happiness—or, ironically, hers.

Since her son was in heaven, beyond her clutching, she could never have him as she desired. So she preferred to nurse her anger in hell rather than release him to be a person on his own.

Angry Words and the Loss of Civility

Noting that good anger expresses itself in gallant deeds rather than in seething words, Lewis isolated an important distinction between good and bad anger. As Tirian told Eustace in *The Last Battle,* "Do not scold, like a kitchen-girl. No warrior scolds. Courteous words or else hard knocks are his only language."[22]

Cowardly anger, self-serving anger, resorts to words hurled from a safe distance that vent our feelings without endangering our lives. "A soft answer turns away wrath, but a harsh word stirs up anger" (Prov. 15:1, NKJV).

Stephen Carter probes these questions in *Civility: Manners, Morals, and the Etiquette of Democracy*, written almost as "a prayer—a prayer for understanding and for our strength, as a nation, to build a society in which we act with, rather than talk about, genuine respect for others."[23]

In a nation filled with "barbarians running late," in which "an astonishing 89 percent of grade school teachers and principals reported that they 'regularly' face abusive language from students,"

Carter wants to restore a civility that "is the sum of the many sacrifices we are called to make for the sake of living together."[24]

Carter relies on the wisdom of Desiderius Erasmus, whose *De Civilitate Morum Puerilium (On Civility in Children)* made it clear that "barbarians" are folks who cannot restrain their passions, while civilized people practice self-discipline. We must follow behavioral standards, decency and courtesy to live well with others. Practicing good manners is one way we love each other.

The loss of civility, Carter thinks, began in 1965, the year this nation became "postmodern."[25] For all its inadequacies—and Carter acknowledges searing problems such as racial injustice—reams of evidence document how much gentler, more caring, more civil Americans were 40 years ago. But the traditions that preserved peace and made society sound have collapsed under the burden of forces unloosed in the 1960s. Self-expression supplanted self-control; self-esteem surpassed sacrifice. Even journalists engaged in "truly primitive"[26] shouting and name-calling, which subverted civilized discourse.

Angry, anonymous letters illustrate this. A century ago Henry Ward Beecher was one of the most prominent men in America. Weekly he preached to thousands in New York City's Plymouth Church. One Sunday he found a letter containing one word: "Fool." He strode to the pulpit and told the people about it: "I have known many an instance of a man writing a letter and forgetting to sign his name, but this is the only instance I have ever known of a man signing his name and forgetting to write the letter."[27]

If only all of us could respond to criticism with Beecher's humor! But even humor cannot undo the harm done by harsh words, critical comments, and malicious gossip.

Certainly we're "languaging" creatures! Jesus said some folks with eyes do not see, and some people with ears do not hear. He never said some people with tongues don't speak! We certainly keep our mouths in motion. And for many of us, our tongues seem to run fastest when our brains are idling! An elderly man said, "Many of us are like a pair of old shoes—all worn out but the tongue."

The Jewish Talmud tells of a king who sent two court jesters on a mission. "Foolish Simon," the king said, "go and bring back the best thing in the world. And you, Silly John, find me the worst thing in the world." Both jesters departed and quickly returned with a package. Simon bowed before the king, saying, "Behold, Sire, the best thing in the world." His package contained a human tongue. Silly John then snickered and undid his package, saying, "The worst thing in the world, Sire!" Another human tongue!

So we've been given the best—and the worst—thing in the world: a tongue. How will we use it?

Lewis suggests, "Reasonableness and amiability (both cheerful 'habits' of the mind) are stronger in the end than the . . . spleen. To rail is the sad privilege of the loser."[28] To walk with Jesus, to talk as Jesus talks, means to let His love, present in the power of His Holy Spirit, free us from resentment and deliver us from the temptation to use our tongues as destructive weapons.

Controlling the tongue seems humanly impossible—and it is. Only the new covenant, in which God puts His law in our hearts, enables us to speak in a Christlike manner.

Now when we think about what Jesus says, most of us despair of ever doing what He urges. How can anyone live like this? That's what He wants us to discover. On our own, we never will!

In Matt. 5:20 Jesus said, "Unless your righteousness surpasses that of the Pharisees and the teachers of the law, you will certainly not enter the kingdom of heaven." So how are we to get into heaven? Only by His gracious assistance. To live as Jesus wants us to, we must learn, with Brother Lawrence, that "when an occasion of practicing some virtue offered, he addressed himself to God, saying, *Lord, I cannot do this unless thou enablest me;* and that then he received strength more than sufficient."[29]

This is why, Stephen Carter believes, religious people, seeking to love God and humanity, living out their faith, possess "the most powerful language of sacrifice and aspiration the human race has ever known."[30]

"I doubt that we can reconstruct civility in America without a revival of religion as a force in both our public and our private lives, because religion can give believers the power to resist the dangerous, self-seeking moral understandings that are coming to dominate our social life."[31] So churches must seriously accept their charge to civilize children.

"Religions do their greatest service to civility when they

preach not only love of neighbor but resistance to wrong."[32] Despite the efforts by secularists to skirt religious issues and sideline religious believers, people of faith must keep the faith, even when it proves costly.

4 ✍ Lust

"Perversions of the Sex Instinct Are Numerous"

Eros "ceases to be a devil only when it ceases to be a god."[1]

WE NORMALLY PREFER PLEASURE TO PAIN. We enjoy fulfilling our biologically based appetites. And of all our desires, the hunger for sexual pleasure is the hardest to control. Historian Will Durant noted, in the first volume of *Story of Civilization,* "The greatest task of morals is always sexual regulation; for the reproductive instinct creates problems not only within marriage, but before and after it, and threatens at any moment to disturb the social order with its persistence, its intensity, its scorn of law, and its perversions."[2] If we stroll with historians through human history, Durant's observation holds: at the core of our story stands the blessing and curse of sex!

A Pervasive Problem

One of the greatest human goods is marriage and family. In the very beginning, "God created man in his own image, in the image of God he created him; male and female he created them" (Gen. 1:27). The two sexes satisfied the Creator's plan, for "the LORD God said, 'It is not good that man should be alone; I will make him a helper comparable to him'" (2:18, NKJV). Consequently, Adam rejoiced, saying, "'This is now bone of my bones and flesh of my flesh; She shall be called Woman, Because she was taken out of Man.' Therefore a man shall leave his father and mother and be joined to his wife, and they shall

53

become one flesh. And they were both naked, the man and his wife, and were not ashamed" (vv. 23-25, NKJV).

Then sin disrupted the bliss of Eden. Infidelity and assorted perversions eventually shattered the goodness of marriage and family, for sin always vandalizes what is good. Sadly enough, sexual sins still shred one of the great goods God designed for humanity: lifelong intimacy, children, and family ties.

Sexual perversions abound wherever people seek to escape God's mandates. Pornography seduces serial killers. Prostitution reduces women to commodities, whose flesh is bought and sold without concern for the people involved. Incest and sexual abuse destroy natural bonds between parents and children. Promiscuity spreads sexually transmitted diseases, incubating epidemics that spread infertility and death.

All of this, of course, C. S. Lewis knew. Entering adolescence, Lewis had a "dancing mistress," who he said was "the first woman I ever 'looked upon to lust after her'; assuredly through no fault of her own."[3] Interestingly, she was not as physically attractive as one of his cousins, whom he remembered as "the most beautiful woman I have ever seen, perfect in shape and color and voice and every movement—but who can describe beauty?"[4]

Unlike his healthy appreciation for his cousin's feminine allure, "What I felt for the dancing mistress was sheer appetite; the prose and not the poetry of the Flesh. I did not feel at all like a knight devoting himself to a lady; I was much more like a Turk looking at a Circassian whom he could not afford to buy. I knew quite well what I wanted."[5]

Despite this early acknowledgment of lust's power, one of his friends, Neville Coghill, noted that in their early years together at Oxford University Lewis rarely talked about sexual issues. His written works rarely accentuate lust and sexual sins. Sins of the spirit, to him, were far more deadly than the sins of the flesh, which are rooted in weakness rather than malice. Yet he occasionally noted lust's magnetic power and damning consequences.

At the beginning of Lewis's *The Pilgrim's Regress*, the book's central character, John (who seems to speak for the author), awakened to a deep inner hunger for "the beautiful Island," something that would satisfy his heart's deepest longings. In his quest, he first explored an adjacent woods, momentarily entranced by nature's beauty. He enjoyed it, but it failed to genuinely satisfy him. He wanted more than delightful seas and sunsets, enchanting cliffs and roses.

Then suddenly, "In the grass beside him sat a laughing brown girl of about his own age, and she had no clothes on." She drew near, seductively stirring his lust. "'It was me you wanted,' said the brown girl. 'I am better than your silly Islands.'" Aroused by her flesh, boldened by her beckoning, "John rose and caught her, all in haste, and committed fornication with her in the wood."[6]

This he did repeatedly, and the woods were soon filled with a brood of brown girls, his own progeny. Ultimately appalled at the consequences of his behavior, John left the woods and began his spiritual journey, aware that his early sexual indulgences could never satisfy his inner discontent. But, irresponsibly, he had called into being little beings—more than he had anticipated. Such is the harvest of lust, another of the seven deadly sins.

This led Lewis to declare, "Chastity is the most unpopular of the Christian virtues. . . . the old Christian rule is, Either marriage, with complete faithfulness to your partner, or else total abstinence."[7] Lust is evil because it subverts chastity; it destroys what's truly good for us, a lasting marriage.

Lust Defined

To understand Jesus' warning against lust, we must carefully define it. First of all, lust is not normal, healthy sexual desire. If you're a man and get no pleasure out of seeing a pretty woman, you're not saintly—you're probably not well. If you're a woman and you don't check out a handsome hulk, you're not particularly pious—you probably have dormant hormones!

What Jesus condemned is a desire that, like anger, seeks to dominate, to use, to manipulate another person for our own pleasure. "Both anger and lust put other people down, though by seemingly polar opposite emotions—by hatred and desire," writes Dale Bruner. "People are used in both."[8]

Lust is *self-serving sensuality*. A literal translation of the New Testament Greek clarifies the meaning of Jesus' condemnation: "Everyone who looks on a woman in order to lust for her has committed adultery with her in his heart."

In William Barclay's judgment, "The man whom Jesus here condemns is the man who deliberately uses his eyes to stimulate his desires; the man who finds a strange delight in things which waken the desire for the forbidden thing."[9]

To Augustine, "That means whosoever fixes his attention on her [we would say "leers at her" or "looks lewdly at her"] with the aim and intention of lusting after her"—that's to say he reduces her to a *thing,* an object—sins. Such a man is not interested in the woman's name or her inner self; he just wants to enjoy himself at her expense. "This is not the same as the experience of sexual passion, the sensation of carnal pleasure," Augustine says. Certainly it's not lustful to feel sexy or to enjoy sexual contact. Without a healthy sex drive, few of us would marry or have kids! However, Augustine insists that lust willfully assents to an illicit liaison, "giving of such full consent that the aroused desire for it is not repressed, but would be satisfied if opportunity presented itself."[10]

We lust for a person when—and only when—we inwardly consent to "doing it" with him or her if given the opportunity. As Thomas Aquinas says, "For with God the intention is taken for the deed."

The great "golden-mouthed" preacher of the Eastern Church, John Chrysostom, spoke clearly when he insisted that Jesus "said not simply 'whosoever shall desire,' since it is possible for one to desire even when sitting in the mountains; but, 'whosoever shall look to lust;' that is to say, he who gathers in lust unto himself; he who, when nothing compels him, brings in the wild beast upon his thoughts when they are calm. For this comes no longer of nature, but of self-indulgence."[11]

We're sexual beings, strongly desiring sexual fulfillment and elated by the pleasures of intercourse. Pleasure may well have been more intense before Adam's fall. Obviously some Christians have prudishly minimized the goodness and ecstasy of sex, but, to Lewis, true Christianity celebrates the body. God himself assumed a body, became flesh. And we will have resurrected bodies in heaven. Too often, however, legitimate sexual pleasure gets wrenched from its rightful context, unhinged from its proper constraints—like a ship's propeller severed by a hidden reef—and the pleasures of sex rapidly corrode and destroy.

That's when sexual desire, so alluring and apparently innocent at its inception, ultimately raises its ugly head as lust.

Lewis I think, would have fully approved this recent definition: "LUST is disordered desire for or inordinate enjoyment of sexual pleasure. Sexual pleasure is morally disordered when sought for itself, isolated from its procreative and unitive purposes."[12] As he observed, people generally eat food for nourishment rather than turning it into a fetish of some sort. Food "perverts" rarely attend "striptease clubs" to see food unveiled. "But perversions of the sex instinct are numerous, hard to cure, and frightful."[13]

The "Sexual Revolution"

What Lewis warned against in the 1940s, an American professor of psychology, Jess Lair, witnessed in the 1960s and 1970s. Perversions of the sex instinct fueled the "sexual revolution," which significantly altered the behavior standards of many young people. Arriving on university campuses, scores of young men and women celebrated their liberation from family and church, joyously entering sexual liaisons with whoever seemed at hand. To "shack up" with a series of "lovers" seemed marvelous to them. Freedom meant freely having sex without the liabilities of lasting vows.

For a time, Lair observed, all this "free sex" seemed totally satisfactory. When a person is 18 or 19 years old, a certain euphoria gilds the one-night stands or living-together relationships. But the passing years, like sand pouring into the bottom of an hourglass, slowly silted burdens that saddled the "liberated" ones with unexpected difficulties. Increasingly, as they moved into their late 20s, "free love" devotees flocked to Lair's office, needing counsel. When the wrinkle-free skin of youth sagged and a person's attractiveness declined a bit, the sex game lost its thrill. After the emotions aroused in sexual encounters were repeatedly crushed, people wondered why sex didn't offer more than they were finding in the act.

Lair states in his book *Sex: If I Didn't Laugh I'd Cry* that what makes sex good is commitment and fidelity, not promiscuous sleeping around. A recent poll of people in their 20s conducted by Rutgers University sums up their attitudes as "sex without strings, relationships without rings."[14]

Lost: Modesty

Certainly such attitudes prevail on trendy college campuses. Wendy Shalit's *A Return to Modesty: Discovering the Lost Virtue*[15] describes her experience at Williams College. Attending one of America's premier liberal arts colleges, ever current with its co-ed dorms and bathrooms, she felt outraged by her peers' sexual permissiveness. She was even more offended by what her elders' "sexual revolution" had dumped on her generation. Casual sex was, in many ways, institutionally encouraged. During Women's Pride Week, for example, the college's feminist association distributed "Shameless Hussy" stickers that female students were urged to wear on their clothing, making it clear they were ready for sexual contacts. Then a billboard advertising "Peer Health" urged the women to drop by and "see our new oral-sex how-to guides."[16] Students clearly heard the message that sex was no big deal.

But a few weeks later young women orchestrated "The Clothesline Project"—and it seemed as though sex was a rather big deal after all! Women stamped messages on T-shirts declaring "Don't touch me again" and "I hate you," or "Why does this keep happening to me?" and "When will this end?"[17] Adding to the darkness occluding the campus were the many women struggling with eating disorders, numbing out on Prozac, and engaging in various forms of self-mutilation. All the casual sex—all the one-night encounters—exacted an anguished toll. As one of Shalit's correspondents asserted, *"Casual* sex is the world's biggest oxymoron!"[18]

To understand why all this was happening, Shalit seriously studied thinkers ancient and modern, especially concerned to grasp why feminists have supported a movement that has so deeply damaged her generation. Why would a feminist columnist such as Camille Paglia advocate *"more* pornography, *better* pornography. Pornography everywhere!"[19] Why would Katie Roiphe, after interviewing Beverly LaHaye's press secretary—a Christian woman who refused to engage in premarital sex—admit that the woman has "a certain glow" that rather "resembles happiness," but declare herself "infuriated" by such an unfashionable commitment to chastity?[20] Why would Simone de Beauvoir, architect of the women's liberation movement, praise the perverse Marquis de Sade as a great moralist?[21] How could Kathryn Harrison in *The Kiss* write about having sex with her father as if nothing were wrong with such perversion? Why would Naomie Wolfe, a highly paid consultant for former United States Vice President Al Gore, declare in her *Promiscuities* that "there are no good girls; we are all bad girls" who should "explore the shadow slut who walks alongside us."[22]

Rationalizations Abound

Pondering such questions, E. Michael Jones focuses on the philosophical foundations for modern sexual behavior and argues, "There are only two alternatives in the intellectual life: either one conforms desire to the truth or one conforms truth to desire."[23] Since our sexual desire is quite powerful, we often rationalize our sexual behavior rather than living as we should.

Though sexual sin does great harm, the "most insidious corruption" to which we fall prey is "the corruption of the mind" that accompanies the process of rationalizing it. "One moves all too easily from sexual sins, which are probably the most common to mankind, to intellectual sins, which are the most pernicious."[24] That process, evident in some of this century's most influential intellectuals, leads Jones to declare, "The verdict is clear: modernity is rationalized lust."[25]

Lust, as Isidore of Seville wrote long ago, dominates the person "who is debauched with pleasures."[26] Thomas Aquinas added that sexual "pleasures above all debauch a man's mind."[27] When sexual desires control a person and debauch his or her mind, he or she easily rationalizes lust. This is evident in psychoanalysis, formed by the obsessions of its founder, Sigmund Freud, which stamps modernity like a seared if fading trademark. Freud's philosophy runs counter to Christianity. And some of Freud's most significant theories—the Oedipus complex, totemism, primitive sexual promiscuity—have no basis in historical or anthropological fact. In fact, "the oldest and ethnologically most primitive people," E. Michael Jones says, followed religions with "striking similarities to both Judaism and Christianity in that these people tend to be monotheistic and monogamous, and even refer to God as 'Our Father.'"[28]

Yet Freud and his devotees have shaped the modern academic world, and young people are inundated with sexually oriented courses and encouraged to promiscuously practice "safe sex."

Hedonism Revived: "The Crisis of Our Age"

However questionable their intellectual sources, today's university students, living out the creed of hedonistic societies, pursue an unrestrained sensuality that is frequently justified by "psychological" experts. Thinking they're avant-garde, they are in fact unearthing an ancient creed. Centuries before Christ, some Greek thinkers called Cyreniacs asserted that the good life is simply the pleasurable life of sexual indulgence, endless entertainments, and alcoholic intoxication—"wine, women, and song."

Today, varieties of hedonism dance across our television sets, leap from magazine ads, lace the lyrics of hit tunes, and proclaim the basic theme: "If it feels good, do it." Whatever gives us pleasure, hedonists declare, deserves doing. Such social currents deeply distressed one of C. S. Lewis's contemporaries, Harvard sociologist Pitrim A. Sorokin.[29] In a probing study, *The American Sex Revolution,* published in 1956, he declared, "Our civilization has become so preoccupied with sex that it now oozes from all pores of American life."[30]

Lust masquerades as love, and that's its gravest threat. Lust effectively depersonalizes other people, depriving them of love. Lust drives us to "love her and leave her," to take no responsibility for the well-being or future of our lust's object.

In Lewis's view, lust, as a warm-blooded sin, is often recognized and repented of. We find in *The Great Divorce* a memorable struggle that finally liberates a ghost from hell—the only one delivered. After visiting the foothills of heaven, this ghost, with "a little red lizard" on his shoulder, is ready to return to hell, where he can pursue the lizard's promptings. Then the "flaming Spirit—an angel, as I now understood" offered to quiet the lizard's voice, to kill it. The ghost demurs, wanting something less "drastic" to deliver him from the lizard's incessant hounding. Like an obese diabetic insisting on "just a bit" of ice cream for dessert, the ghost wanted something more "gradual," but the angel insisted that only the lizard's death would accomplish what's truly good for him.

After a lengthy inner struggle, the ghost at last permitted the angel to do his work, even allowing that it might kill both him and the lizard. Contritely he confessed, "It would be better to be dead than to live with this creature." Submitting to God's will, he asked for His help. Suddenly, "the Ghost gave a scream of agony such as I never heard on Earth. The Burning One closed his crimson grip on the reptile: twisted it, while it bit and writhed, and then flung it, broken backed, on the turf."[31]

Then a miracle occurred. The lizard, slain by the angel, was transformed into a great horse, "the greatest stallion I have ever seen, silvery white but with mane and tail of gold."[32] The former ghost, freed from the power of lust, mounted the stallion and rode heavenward toward the mountains. Explaining to Lewis what had transpired, George Macdonald says,

> Nothing, not even the best and noblest, can go on as it now is. Nothing, not even what is lowest and most bestial, will not be raised again if it submits to death. It is sown a natural body, it is raised a spiritual body. Flesh and blood cannot come to the Mountains. Not because they are too rank, but because they are too weak. What is a Lizard compared with a stallion? Lust is a poor, weak, whispering thing compared with that richness and energy of desire which will arise when lust has been killed.[33]

The sensuality of the hedonism so evident in the *Playboy* ethos results from wrongly satisfying healthy physical desires. To this, Lewis and the apostle Paul would respond,

> For this is the will of God, your sanctification: that you should abstain from sexual immorality; that each of you should know how to possess his own vessel in sanctification and honor, not in passion of lust, like the Gentiles who do not know God; that no one would take advantage of and defraud his brother in this matter, because the Lord is the avenger of all such, as we also forewarned you and testified. For God did not call us to uncleanness, but in holiness (*1 Thess. 4:3-7, NKJV*).

5 ✍ Gluttony

"Her Belly Dominates Her Whole Life"

Mere excess in food is much less valuable than delicacy. . . . . On that, as on every other subject, keep your man in a condition of false spirituality.[1]

MOST OF US WHO WORK WITH COMPUTERS know the cardinal rule of computer programming: Garbage in, garbage out. Physiologically, the same rule applies: "We are what we eat"—garbage in, garbage out. Whatever we ingest—physically, intellectually, or spiritually—we digest. And what we digest seeps slowly but surely into what we are. Our eating—what we eat and how we eat, what we drink and how we drink—shapes our being.

Thus medieval thinkers linked the sins of gluttony and lust, for both illustrate our frequent failures to control our physical appetites. Lewis noted that even the most rigorous Christian asceticism demanded a balanced appreciation for the goodness of creation and its physical pleasures. Even self-denying monks realized, "Marriage is good, though not for me; wine is good, though I must not drink it; feasts are good, though today we fast."[2]

Thomas Aquinas defined gluttony as "immoderate desire" in eating and drinking. Anything is immoderate, he thought, that discards "the order of reason, wherein the good of moral virtue consists."[3] Centuries earlier, Pope Gregory I classified "the vice of gluttony" in five ways. "Sometimes it forestalls the hour of need; sometimes it seeks costly meats; sometimes it requires the food to be daintily cooked; sometimes it exceeds the measure of refreshment by taking too much; sometimes we sin by the very heat of an immoderate appetite." Gregory pointed out that we eat wrong when we eat "hastily, sumptuously, too much, greedily, daintily."[4]

So let's follow Gregory's list of gluttony's five-sided temptation and see how Lewis's works supply suitable illustrations of this deadly sin.

Hastily: Gulping to Taste More

Early in *The Lion, the Witch, and the Wardrobe*, the Pevensie children meet the "White Witch," who ruled Narnia. She recognized them as the first wave of invaders, sent by Aslan, to reclaim Narnia. So she tried to entice them in various ways, especially by feeding one of the children, Edmund, "Turkish Delight," the sweetest treat imaginable. Edmund found the taste quite unforgettable, and his desire for Turkish Delight soon led him to betray the little band.

Gluttony is a deadly sin because it so easily leads us to exchange essentially good things for things that superficially taste good. Young Edmund couldn't enjoy the simple, tasty fare (fresh fish, potatoes, butter, milk, rolls) offered to him by Mrs. Beaver, who, with her husband, risked her life to provide shelter for the children. While feasting on plain fare, *good* food, he fantasized about "Turkish Delight—and there's nothing that spoils the taste of good ordinary food half so much as the memory of bad magic food."[5]

He'd found himself a god that would destroy the goodness of true pleasure and himself as well.

In time, he became obsessed by memories of Turkish Delight. He couldn't keep his mind off it. His longing to have more from the queen's magic bottle prompted him to slip away from his companions and betray the Beavers so he could have some more sweets.

Gluttony, so focused on filling itself, excludes gratitude, the giving away of self. In fact, one of the true indicators of gluttony is the lack of thanksgiving. When Edmund succumbed to Turkish Delight's addictive lure, he went looking for the witch to satiate his appetite. When she met him, she magically made pounds of the sweet potion. Edmund gorged himself and felt serenely con-

tent. So absorbed did he become in eating that he failed to fathom the queen's questions.

His desire for Turkish Delight rendered him as helpless as
soft concrete in the White Witch's hands. Her inquiries unveiled
the whereabouts of his friends. He betrayed them. He fell victim
to what Gilbert Meilaender labels "The Sweet Poison of the
False Infinite," failing to live temperately, treating created things
with "neither worship nor contempt." Throughout the Narnian
chronicles, Meilaender argues, we encounter profound evoca-
tions of this theme. Edmund's addiction to Turkish Delight,
gulping down more than he needed, gives us the "key" to understanding the insatiable, addictive nature of gluttony.[6] He was
willing to do anything—even to betray his friends and family—
to get more sweets.

Conversely, gratitude reveres the giver rather than the gift.
The husband who thanks his wife for cooking a meal, the
woman who thanks her husband for fixing a snack, the family
who thanks God for the trees and plants that provide them apples and beans reflect a holy attitude of gratitude. But gluttons
rarely say grace before meals. They rarely recognize the sheer
givenness, the *graciousness* of sun and sea, potatoes and cattle,
that bring us our food.

Sumptuously: Demanding Rich Foods

In *The Silver Chair*, Lewis tells of two children, Jill Pole and
Eustace Scrubb, who with a "Marsh-wiggle" named Puddleglum
set forth on an adventure, seeking to rescue Narnia's Prince Rilian, who had been abducted by an evil witch.

After nearly freezing to death early on in their journey, they
reached "the house of Harfang," where they took refuge in the
castle belonging to a family of giants. The queen giant ordered
her servants to secure the Narnians' comfort. "Give them food
and wine and baths. . . . Give her lollipops, give her dolls, give
her physics, give all you can think of—possets and comfits and
caraways and lullabies and toys." Then the giant added, with
words Jill didn't fully grasp, "Don't cry, little girl, or you won't
be good for anything when the feast comes."[7]

Jill was taken to a huge room with a "giant foot bath," where
she relaxed in warm water and delighted in clean clothes. Then

she enjoyed a marvelous meal, including "hot roast turkey, and a steamed pudding, and roast chestnuts, and as much fruit as you could eat."[8] Topping it all off, she was tucked into a soft bed and was soon dead to the world. Had not Aslan, the Lion, dramatically appeared to her and reminded her of the "signs" she was supposed to daily repeat, she might have been lulled into such comfort that she and her friends would have become, as the giants desired, tasty morsels for their feast.

Jill and her friends discovered what we too often ignore. When we're too comfortable, too easily lulled to sleep by food and drink, we often fail to follow God's will, and we slip into the grip of spiritual giants intent on destroying us.

We forget that the Christian tradition warns that simply to live and eat sumptuously—lavishly, opulently, extravagantly—subtly subverts our will to live virtuously.

Too Much: Excessive Amounts

We clearly struggle to restrain our hungers! Many of us are overweight. People with more than 30 percent body fat are labeled obese by health experts, and *three-fourths* of us older than 25 *are* obese. Alarming numbers of schoolchildren, riding their school busses and playing video games, are overweight and out of shape.

Obesity, like a fifth column betraying us from within, triggers heart disease, strokes, diabetes. Some folks die young because they use tobacco, eat poorly, abuse alcohol, and refuse to exercise. We're slowly killing ourselves.

Yet paradoxically, in our affluent society other people struggle with anorexia and bulimia—eating disorders focused on denying needed nutrients from one's diet. And if we turn on the television set, we note charity specials and nightly newscasts that remind us how many millions of people in our world go hungry every day.

In a *Christianity Today* article, "The Fatted Faithful," Virginia Stem Owens reflects on a study showing that religious people are more obese than other people. While we see no clear explanation for the correlation, the study's author suggests Christians draw clear lines against such things as using tobacco and alcohol but rarely consider gluttony as particularly sinful. Especially in our day of unconditional love and the nonjudgmental acceptance of everyone, few preachers would suggest that gluttony might endanger our souls!

Interestingly enough, Owens herself does the same, ending the article by lightly dismissing the issue, referring to a saintly friend of hers who is quite overweight, concluding that since it has not hindered her walk with Christ, it must not be worth worrying about![9]

Owens reflects the mood of modern Evangelicalism, with its general disinterest in costly self-disciplines. But C. S. Lewis warned against such self-serving arguments, and he knew how such soft evasions harm the true faith. He understood Satan's nearly total triumph in today's world, persuading even the saints that gluttony is at worst a weakness that poses no eternal questions.

In an insightful passage of *The Screwtape Letters*, Screwtape sharply rebukes his nephew Wormwood for dismissing gluttony as a serious sin. In fact, dulling folks' conscience to its damning dimensions was one of Satan's most recent great advances. Preachers, ever up-to-date, feared to offend plump parishioners and rarely mentioned it, so it's easily indulged, subtly seductive.[10]

Condemnation regularly crackles like static electricity against racism, sexism, social injustice, and economic inequities. Other messages explore ways to find happiness, to avoid worries, to boost self-esteem, to balance jobs and families. But probing peoples' consciences about eating or drinking too much—or watching too much TV or seeing too many movies—would quickly cost such prophets their pulpits.

Greedily: When and Where One Demands

We need food, obviously, and we need the right food—food fit for humans. We can't eat just anything. Goats consume paper, twigs, discarded socks, just about anything. Obviously we're not goats—though some college students I've known come close to being omnivorous! We need food, yet our modern diets, with their fats and sugars and additives, frequently harm us.

We are, in significant ways, what we eat. We need the right kind of food to live right. And good food is available. Few pleasures rival a cold drink when you're thirsty. When depleted of water by vigorous exercise, or sapped of liquid by intense heat, our bodies cry for a drink. To find cool water—or lemonade—after a long hard run gives incomparable pleasure. And when you're hungry, when the cells of your body scream for attention, eating becomes a great pleasure. We like foods that taste good as well as those we know nourish us. Usually our tastes are satisfied when we eat things that do good to our bodies. Even our craving for sweets reflects our need for carbohydrates to fuel our cells. So an occasional slice of pie gives us pleasure and supplies the calories, fat, vitamins, and minerals we need.

If, however, you prefer pie to apples and oranges, and if you eat a whole pie each evening, in 20 years or so doctors will discover that your arteries look like blubber-filled tubes, clogged with sticky rubber cement, causing a slower flow of blood. And if you become so consumed by your love of pie that you eat nothing else every day, eventually an ambulance will roll up to your door to haul away your carcass!

Eating pleases our palates, but unless it's restrained by principled habits, wherein food mainly supplies nutritional needs, the pleasure becomes destructive.

Lewis fully understood gluttony's true nature, the reason for its basic sinfulness. Too often limited to discussions of specific acts—overeating or drunkenness—gluttony actually refers to the abuse of good things. It's more an attitude than an act, more evident in the priorities by which we live than the portions of meat and potatoes we place on our plates. Gluttons crave more than pleasures of the palate—they delight in the *process of consuming* food or drink.

The person who is consumed by consuming, oblivious to all around him or her, grateful for neither the healthy taste or sheer abundance of the food, illustrates gluttony. The pleasure of eating, not nutritional needs or fellowship with friends and family, draws the glutton to the table. Getting food he or she enjoys determines the fare. Just as lust focuses on the one who lusts using others as objects to satisfy sexual cravings, so gluttony focuses on the glutton and the satisfaction of his or her appetites.

Daintily: Perfectly Prepared

Given the abundance surrounding us, many of today's gluttons may be more addicted to what Lewis called the "gluttony of

Delicacy, not gluttony of Excess." Satan's skill in separating us from God was illustrated in *The Screwtape Letters* by a woman, the "patient's mother," whose gluttony was evident in her demands upon people, not the amounts of food she consumed. In time she'd find she'd been a food slave, even though she ate very little. Her obsession with having her food *just right for her* allowed the demonic tempter assigned to her, Glubose, to cradle her soul in his hands, lulling it to sleep with delusions of self-righteousness.

In fact, "She is a positive terror to hostesses and servants. She is always turning from what has been offered her to say with a demure little sigh and a smile, 'Oh, please, please . . . *all* I want is a cup of tea, weak but not too weak, and the teeniest teeniest bit of really crisp toast.'"[11] She wanted very little, but her wants made her a pain to everyone around her. "In a crowded restaurant she gives a little scream at the plate which some overworked waitress has set before her and says: 'Oh, that's far, far too much! Take it away and bring me about a quarter of it.'"[12]

What had happened, Lewis noted, is that this woman's "belly now dominates her whole life."[13] And that's what makes gluttony so damning! When anything—our belly or our sexuality or our pride—dominates us, everything is lost.

Lewis's point is that gluttony makes satisfying a person's desire for food a ruling theme in his or her life. Neither the quantity nor variety of food consumed is the real issue. Gluttony makes satisfying our own appetites more important than anything else. And, typical of sin in general, it isolates us from loving contact with God and humanity.

In our society gluttony may be more evident in fastidious diets than in excess consumption. Health food addicts and physical fitness fanatics often illustrate gluttony at its worst. Vegetarians, imposing their dietary standards on families and friends, easily embrace gluttony. As Henry Fairlie notes, "Those who take too fastidious an interest in themselves seldom have the time or the inclination to take much interest in anyone else. They are consumed with self-love. When their eyes are not on the bathroom scales, they are on the mirror."[14] Modern physical fitness centers, which attract throngs of young (and want-to-be-young) adults, frequently feature mirrored walls. Apparently the patrons want to watch themselves in action! Health food stores, frequently offering exotic items guaranteed to insure immortality, feature high prices as well as soaring promises. A legitimate concern for health leads to diligent exercise and nutritious food, but intemperance beckons when diet and fitness control a person's life.

Gluttony's "Daughters"

Gluttony also has "daughters," according to Gregory the Great.[15] Thomas Aquinas explored the spiritual implications of the vice, finding it responsible for a certain "dullness of sense in the understanding." Abstinence, conversely, contributes to the penetrating power of wisdom. "I thought in my heart to withdraw my flesh from wine, that I might turn my mind in wisdom" (Eccles. 2:3).[16] When we've just eaten a meal, our brains slow down as the stomach demands extra energy to digest the food. We often want a nap. Too much food seems to clog the brain. More seriously, alcohol and drugs easily disable our minds.

So we find, in Lewis's *The Silver Chair*, Jill and Scrubb and Puddleglum enter an underground "Dark Castle," where an evil witch has imprisoned Rilian, Prince of Narnia. They free him from his bondage in the Silver Chair, but the witch prevents their escape by tossing "green powder" on the fire in their chamber. "It did not blaze much, but a very sweet and drowsy smell came from it."[17] As they inhaled, they found it "harder to think," and lapsed into lethargy. Suitably drugged, they began to doubt basic truths, even wondering if there was indeed a place called Narnia. Finally, the witch insisted, "There never was such a world,"[18] and the children agreed.

When we're too full, when we're intoxicated by liquor, when we're addicted to mind-numbing drugs, we easily forget our real home. We forget we've come from God and soon must meet Him. We live so immersed in the deadening delights of food and drink and comfort that we fail to awaken to our everlasting destiny.

Turning again to Aquinas, we read that a "disordered" appetite, immoderately eating and drinking, deadens our reason and persuades us that we have found something good. Wine, he notes, falsely "gives every one a confident and joyful mind."[19]

As Proverbs reminds us, "Be not among winebibbers; among riotous eaters of flesh: For the drunkard and the glutton shall come to poverty: and drowsiness shall clothe a man with rags" (Prov. 23:20-21, KJV). We are by nature rational creatures, and we must resist anything that decreases our rational powers. Excess food, intoxicating drink, mind-altering drugs, the vices associated with gluttony easily derail reason.

Interestingly enough, Aquinas, seeking the "daughters of gluttony," finds them in speech. He proposes a connection between a person's inability to control his or her desires for food and drink and the inability to curb a tendency to gossip and harm others with his or her words. "Inordinate" words, or "loquaciousness," are as deadly as food and drink. Finally, Aquinas thought gluttony facilitated "scurrility," which is "a kind of levity resulting from lack of reason, which is unable not only to bridle the speech, but also to restrain outward behavior."[20]

Some folks think getting a laugh is worthwhile regardless of how much it may pain others. Such jocularity, while giving a person certain visibility and even popularity, easily turns sinful. Excessive speech, too many words, saying anything necessary to entertain others hardens one's soul and may be understood as a form of gluttony.

Overconsumption: Environmental Ills

Underlying much of modernity is a philosophical materialism, a collective gluttony, which has transformed us into something horrible—consumers. We consume creation the way we consume fat, for pleasure rather than life. Amid the tumult of the technological revolution, Lewis sided with romantics such as J. R. R. Tolkien and protested the travesties occurring as bulldozers and steam shovels redesigned the earth.

In *That Hideous Strength*, Lewis portrayed a voracious clique, utterly corrupted by sin, willing to devour planet earth to establish its utopian world. One of the story's villains, Lord Feverstone, envisioned a scientifically orchestrated, governmentally supported utopia. He told his young associate, Mark, that a new world was needed—and men like himself could make it.

Sanitizing eugenic programs would be used to cleanse the planet of riffraff and other deficient people. A "new man" would emerge and preside over a planet cleansed of all vegetation.

Rather than being encultured by the virtue tradition of Western Christian culture, the new world will be ruled by what Lewis labeled "Conditioners." Such rulers will exploit people's physical desires, responding to "their felt emotional weight at a given moment,"[21] scratching them where they itch. Deprived of objective standards by their education, people will come to view as all truth and morality their subjective responses to the moment's most powerful impulse. Knowing history well, Lewis doubted that we could find powerful folks who "stepped outside traditional morality" and "used that power benevolently."[22]

Like lust, gluttony abuses and misuses the goodness of creation. Rather than simply accepting food and drink as good gifts from God on His terms, gluttony clutches them as entitlements to be used as one wishes. This attitude easily seduces us to turn our backs on God and is a deadly sin because it can undermine the character we need to persevere on our journey to God. "The good man eats to live, while the evil man lives to eat" (Prov. 13:25, TLB).

6 ✎ Sloth

"This Made It Hard to Think"

*Nothing else was responsible for it [his delay
in answering letter] except the perpetual labour
of writing and (lest I should seem to exonerate
myself too much) a certain Accidia [sloth],
an evil disease and, I believe, of the Seven Deadly
Sins one which in me is the strongest—
though few believe this of me.*[1]

SLACK SELF-DISCIPLINE, like an immobilized muscle, usually underlies the lack of spiritual health and holiness in many Christians' lives. We're all familiar with the slick slogans many embrace: *Hang loose! Go with the flow! Don't get uptight! Live and let live! I'm OK—you're OK! Don't worry—be happy!*

"I do my thing, and you do your thing," intones Fritz Perls in a Gestalt ecstasy. "You are you, and I am I, and if by chance we find each other, it's beautiful."[2] We're ever encouraged to plaster over our anxieties by mouthing such bromides. Much that goes under the banner of "pop psychology" slides swiftly into jargon-style sloth, for whenever we're urged to "accept ourselves as we are," avoiding all challenges to our settled ways of living, we get lazy. To settle into our comfort zones, to "accept ourselves just as we are," rather than work to remedy our deficiencies, soothes us into an indolent and dangerous security.

But discipleship includes *discipline,* and we must overcome sloth to be holy. Without spiritual disciplines, rooted in love for God and humanity, holiness eludes us like a desert mirage.

The Way of "Mr. Halfways"

The main character in Lewis's *The Pilgrim's Regress*, John, discovered this soon after he began his journey in quest of the "Island" he had envisioned. "Mr. Halfways" told John that the Island, the Source of the Joy that forever allured him, could be discovered anywhere. No need to exercise his body and mind on a demanding journey to the Promised Land—he need only shift his perspective. Rarely ethereal, joy's found "everywhere and nowhere." Anyone can find it, for it's all a state of mind, an inner reality easily attained.

When John objected, demanding objective "truth" rather than mental peace, Mr. Halfways resurrected Pilate's skepticism, asking "What is truth?" and taking refuge in his private projections on the screen of subjectivity.

Later on his journey, John and his companion, Vertue, meet "Mr. Sensible," whose prescription for the good life included constant self-indulgence. After listening to him, Vertue discerned that his "art" appeared to equate happiness with untroubled circumstances and unending delight. His parting words to the pilgrims were *"Viva la bagatelle! . . . Do what you will."*[3] Everyone finds his or her own way, writes his or her own script. Everyone's right, and only intolerance is intolerable.

"Tolerate anything except intolerance!" How familiar these words sound, for we find in many circles tolerance elevated to a cardinal virtue. However, much of the tolerance we find is little more than sloth!

"In the world it is called Tolerance, but in hell it is called Despair," said one of Lewis's friends, Dorothy Sayers. "It is the sin that believes in nothing, cares for nothing, seeks to know nothing, interferes with nothing, enjoys nothing, hates nothing, finds purpose in nothing, lives for nothing, and remains alive because there is nothing for which it will die."[4]

According to one of the church fathers, John of Damascus, sloth is a kind of "oppressive sorrow."[5] Thomas Aquinas adds that it "implies a certain weariness of work . . . a sluggishness of the mind which neglects to begin good."[6] It actually rejects the joy of God and resists His goodness. Like a rebellious child of prosperous parents, sloth prefers poverty to family structures. It's mainly a sin of omission, a numbed quality of soul that delays us from doing what we should do to attain our eternal end. Knowing we should love God and our neighbor, we find and justify ways to avoid doing either.

Laziness, Security

Love works! Love acts! Given the fact that love demands effort, Scott Peck argues in *The Road Less Traveled* that "the essence of nonlove is laziness."[7] He believes laziness is *the* main obstacle to spiritual growth and effective life. In his quest to understand humanity's failures, Peck "became increasingly aware of the ubiquitous nature of laziness."[8] His patients (and Peck himself, he admits) endlessly evade the challenges to take responsibility for life. "A major form that laziness takes is fear," Peck continues.[9]

We fear to accelerate on the freeways of life. We fear to risk climbing high mountains. We ski the safe "bunny slopes" rather than hone our skills on the expert runs. We fear standing out in a crowd, and we fear the criticism that comes when we oppose and denounce evil. So we lapse into trite clichés, rationalizing our passivity, comfortable in our conformity.

We too often choose the *safe* way, the *secure* way. Despite this, however, as John discovers, in *The Pilgrim's Regress,* the way to goodness entails risks and discomforts. The way to heaven is narrow and often constricts us, shaving away extraneous baggage. Toward the end of his journey, noting that "Mother Kirk," the Church, "treats us very ill," leading us in "narrow" and "dangerous" ways, John hears his Guide say, "You all know that security is mortal's greatest enemy."[10]

This desire for security, Lewis thought, easily threatens our moral and spiritual life. In his second space fantasy, *Perelandra,* Lewis draws us into an imaginary planet, a pristine, "warm, maternal, delicately gorgeous world,"[11] where the Green Lady (the new planet's Eve) and Ransom spend their days on ocean-caressed, undulating islands.

Soon after stepping on one of the islands, Ransom tastes the fruit of a mysterious "bubble-tree" and revels in its sweetness. Tempted to take another gourd simply because it tastes so good, he wonders if his "itch to have things over again" might be the "root of all evil." He knows that Scripture identifies it as the "love of money," but he wonders if money is merely a means to an end, mainly valued "as a defense against chance, a security for being able to have things over again, a means of arresting the unrolling of the film."[12]

Soon he meets the Green Lady and ultimately engages in mortal combat with the emissary of evil, the physicist Weston. Listening to Weston's words, the Green Lady is tempted to disobey her Lord, Maleldil, and to leave the floating islands that supply her needs to enjoy security on the Fixed Land. She wrestles with temptation. But Ransom prevails, and she tells Ransom that when the "Evil One" was vanquished she awoke, with a clear mind, and was amazed. Her desire for the Fixed Land was nothing but a desire to take control of her life, to slip away from Maleldil, to avoid the uncertainties of living by faith in his providence and love.

The Green Lady discovers how spiritual struggles, swimming through swirling waters of doubt and uncertainty, strengthens their faith. But rather than join the struggle, many of us ponder ultimate issues as if they are interesting aspects of a table game. We settle into a comfortable sentimentality or cynicism. Beneath the disinterest in eternal issues, we have a devious desire to avoid the difficult thoughts and tasks that make us moral people.

"Jargon, Not Argument"

Ironically, we're tempted to avoid what satisfies our deepest desire. The anxiety festering in our soul is a fear of ultimate nothingness, a slothful cancer that devours us. We veil such dark holes with clichés and proverbs, pretending they add substance to our being. Though the words are empty soap bubbles that burst upon contact with reality, they easily mesmerize us.

In *The Screwtape Letters,* Screwtape tells his nephew Wormwood to use jargon to mislead his subject. Earlier generations followed "arguments," knowing why they believed certain things. Modern media—anecdotal rather than analytical—encourage folks to bundle together "a dozen incompatible philosophies" so that ideas are not true or false but "academic" or "practical," old-fashioned or modern, useful or privileged. "Jargon, not argument, is your best ally in keeping him from the Church."[13]

Following this instruction, Screwtape later urges Wormwood to "keep everything hazy in his mind now," and forever after he could delight when he awakened to the "peculiar kind of clarity which Hell affords."[14] Even when Screwtape suggests using sexual temptation to drag down his target, he cautions Wormwood to remember that mental confusion paves the way for moral misdeeds, that illogic dissolves moral standards.

In one of Lewis's Narnian stories, *The Silver Chair*, Aslan sent two children, Jill Pole and Eustace Scrubb (delivered from their prison of a "progressive school") to rescue Narnia's abducted Prince Rilian. Aslan gave Jill detailed instructions to memorize and routinely repeat four signs that would insure the success of her mission: every morning, every night, the signs must stay locked in her mind. Whatever happens, she must follow the signs.

Such words prod us to remember Yahweh's words to the Israelites, who were commanded, on their way to the Promised Land, to commit His words to their hearts. We know, of course, how routinely the Israelites failed to follow orders. Replicating their sloth, Jill forgot to recite and thus stopped remembering Aslan's signs. Distracted by various adventures, she turned slothful, discontinuing her prescribed disciplines. It's often easier to act than to think, to respond rather than consider what's right. We often fail to handle crises because we've failed to think through how to behave. So, Lewis says, Jill failed to stay attuned to revealed truths.

Ultimately they plunged into an underground chamber and became, along with Prince Rilian, prisoners of an evil witch. She nearly persuaded them that neither the sun nor Aslan actually existed but were figments of their imaginations. Then she tossed some green powder onto the fire and played a mandolin, soothing them to a drowsy state. Her bewitchment left them listless.

Only the dour Marsh-wiggle "Puddleglum was still fighting hard. 'I don't know rightly what you mean by a world,' he said, talking like a man who hadn't enough air. 'But you can play that fiddle till your fingers drop off, and still you won't make me forget Narnia; and the whole Overworld too.'"[15]

His efforts to resist her spell prompted the witch to force-feed some psychological rationalizations. Their ideas about the lion and the sun were simple projections. "You have seen lamps, and so you imagined a bigger and better lamp and called it the *sun*. You've seen cats, and now you want a bigger and better cat, and it's to be called a *lion*. Well, 'tis a pretty make-believe, though, to say truth, it would suit you all better if you were younger."[16]

Puddleglum rallied his energy, and courageously he stuck his hand into the fire.[17] As he anticipated, it hurt! But the pain cleared his head, "and he knew exactly what he really thought."[18] The smell of his burning flesh awakened his comrades, and they began to remember the truths Aslan had entrusted to them. Like liberated captives, they began their own journey to the Light, led along by their memory of Aslan's instructions. Only as they took the initiative to escape the witch's control did they move toward salvation. They overcame the deadening sloth of sin. Their minds had come alive!

Educational Slackness

Lewis believed the devil seeks to keep our minds numb, so he forever infiltrates schools such as the one Jill and Eustace attended—schools flying the flag of "progressive education" in which teachers encourage students' natural bent to self-indulgence, pretending this enables them to "find themselves" or to elevate their self-esteem. The teachers let the students do what they enjoyed. "And unfortunately what ten or fifteen of the biggest boys and girls liked best was bullying the others."[19] Other than learning how to avoid such bullies, "owing to the curious methods of teaching at Experiment House, one did not learn much French or Math or Latin or things of that sort."[20]

Consequently, though the vocabulary of schoolchildren in 1945 amounted to 25,000 words, their counterparts in 1992 had only 10,000 words at their disposal.[21] Despite the fact that money spent for education tripled between 1964 and 1976, student performance, especially in verbal proficiency, slipped sharply. Even college graduates perform poorly when tested on their ability to read and analyze such things as bus schedules and editorial arguments.[22]

C. S. Lewis often thought and wrote on educational topics, and he routinely condemned those who would erase toil and difficulty from learning. He fondly remembered the impact of one of his teachers, W. T. Kirkpatrick, whose challenging questions first forced him to think logically.

Though "Kirk" was an agnostic, Lewis always remembered

him fondly. In a letter written at the news of Kirkpatrick's death, Lewis said he actually owed him "in the intellectual sphere as much as one human being can owe another." Under "Kirk," he entered "an atmosphere of unrelenting clearness and rigid honesty of thought" that led him to assert, "For this I shall be the better for as long as I live."[23] And "the more one sees of weakness, affectation, and general vagueness in the majority of men, the more one admires that rigid, lonely old figure—more like some ancient Stoic standing fast in the Roman decadence than a modern scholar living in the home counties. Indeed we may almost call him a great man."[24]

Kirkpatrick's clarity of expression, rooted in a lifetime of diligent study and thought, contrasted dramatically with the collection of "scholars" at N.I.C.E. in the final volume of Lewis's space trilogy, *That Hideous Strength*. These men had university degrees and knew how to display a facade of jargon, but they were frauds. The only real scholar, Bill "the Buzzard" Hingest, was murdered for his refusal to stay with the organization. In fact, the scholars at N.I.C.E. lived in a literal fog of deceit, and one of the institute's main objectives was to mislead the public with propaganda.

Nothing at N.I.C.E. seemed clear. All edges were blurred; all distinctions, shaded. The place had no solid standards, no absolute truths, no lasting laws. It was as if one's eyes were permanently dilated and unable to focus. Young Mark, unfortunately, was ill-prepared to resist the evil pervading N.I.C.E. His "education" failed him, for he knew little of classical or Christian thought. He was thoroughly *modern,* filled with fragments of information and political correctness, but he "was a man of straw."[25]

Spiritual Sloth

Even more slothful are the spiritual gurus who preach self-actualization in New Age seminars; transcendental meditation; rolfing; or scientology. For sloth, ultimately, is less about lazy students than about pain-free recipes for spiritual growth and perfection. Shortcuts to holiness trade in sloth. All such "spiritualities" dispense with the daily difficulties, the disciplines, the sacrifices necessary for true spiritual health. Shortcuts to sanctity, weekend catharses promising permanent cleansing, offer short circuits to heavenly bliss.

Successful churches too often proclaim an attractive message that warms hearers' hearts. David Frum recently assessed contemporary America, noting that Evangelical and Pentecostal churches have boomed. In their success, however, he sees a "shift from an ethic of rectitude to an ethic of forgiveness." They've found an easier way, a shortcut to heaven. "They hungered for religion's sweets, but rejected religion's discipline; wanted its help in trouble but not the structures that might have kept them out of trouble; expected its ecstasy but rejected its ethics; demanded salvation, but rejected the harsh, antique dichotomy of right and wrong."[26]

That's what Marsha G. Witten found in her study *All Is Forgiven: The Secular Message in American Protestantism*. The "good news" she says, is that the church is ready to "meet your needs in the 1990s."[27] Witten studied a number of sermons and found that most revealed a fundamental accommodation to our secular society. God no longer appears as a holy, absolute Being. He's portrayed as "Daddy, Sufferer, Lover," routinely praised for His "positive" contributions to our well-being. He's a therapist anxious to soothe our souls.

Thus, God is routinely invoked as a "Daddy" who suffers emotional distress when we err. He feels our pain and empathizes with us. That He might actually be incensed by our sin never seems to register with modern preachers. We're assured that He loves us unconditionally and is saddened but not angry with our sinful behavior. He loves us "regardless of merit and in the same way—freely and equally."[28]

Now and then sermons remind people that God is also a "Judge" who will punish unrepentant sinners. But in many pulpits we find the "transcendent, majestic, awesome God of Luther and Calvin" significantly diminished.[29] Today's God, mainly concerned with "his immanence and understanding, smiles benevolently on the age of psychology."[30]

In every person, modern preachers suggest, is an innately good self, created in God's image, which needs deliverance from legalism to find the freedom and joy designed for him or her. Certainly we need God to help us find our real selves, but He's more a facilitator than redeemer.

"Conversion," Witten concludes, "is portrayed far less as the need to grapple with sin-nature than as a reorientation of one's psychology toward the creation of a close interpersonal relationship with God."[31]

Tragically, such a stance easily embraces the "cheap grace" that has subverted Jesus' call to "take up your cross and follow" Him.

Remember: "The desire of the slothful killeth him; for his hands refuse to labour" (Prov. 21:25, KJV).

7 ✍ Avarice

"This Itch to Have Things"

"You all know," said the Guide, "that security is mortal's greatest enemy."[1]

ONE OF PAUL'S HAUNTING LAMENTS refers to a one-time friend and fellow follower of Christ, Demos, who "has forsaken me, having loved this present world" (2 Tim. 4:10, NKJV). Demos's love for the world and its comforts reveals the seventh deadly sin: covetousness, greed, avarice. This is the sin condemned by the 10th commandment, which restrains one's desire for wealth and its power over others.

Loving things easily excludes love for persons. So covetousness circulates like a parasitic bacterium, infecting all that is evil—just as love is a fragrance that infuses all good.

The Hebrew word for coveting means to "desire, yearn for, lust after" something so as to gratify one's self. It's a strong word, earmarking the assent by which a person launches a process to attain his or her ends.

The process begins with an *assent* to a plan. The Latin word *avaritia* means greed, and a Latin phrase that succinctly describes it is *libido dominandi*—a will to power, an intent to get, control, and use things that aren't ours. Avarice, like a renegade rancher, seeks to stamp its searing brand on every calf in sight, indifferent to its true owner.

This is evident, Thomas Aquinas wrote, when "a man obtains money beyond his due, by stealing or retaining another's property," unjustly getting what he has no right to have. But it also involves, he continued, an immoderate inner hunger for wealth. It shows when a person burns within—and burns the candle at both ends—wanting "riches too much, or takes too much pleasure in them, even if he be unwilling to steal."[2]

More than mere wishful thinking, more than "Who wants to be a millionaire?" daydreaming, coveting involves taking specific steps—even if only in our minds—to get what we desire. Like lust, avarice involves an assent of the will to the imagination's aspiration.

Though we often think "coveting" refers only to houses and lands, it applies to all of life, especially our desire to control people and organizations as well as to accumulate possessions. It's a deadly sin that threatens our soul, for as George Macdonald noted, "If it be *things* that slay you, what matter whether things you have, or things you have not?"[3]

"Carrying His Torture"

In *The Great Divorce*, Lewis illustrates just how deadly avarice becomes when one of the "ghosts," a "bowler-hatted" fellow called Ikey, on an excursion from hell discovered a tree with golden apples. Just imagine—a pure gold apple tree! Overcoming various obstacles, Ikey went to the tree and huddled in its shade. A gust of wind dislodged some apples, which struck and injured him. "But soon he was at work again. I could see him feverishly trying to fill his pockets with the apples. Of course it was useless."[4]

They were too heavy, and he, a ghost, was too insubstantial to carry much. Failing to fill his pockets, he tried unsuccessfully to lift two apples. Still struggling, he tried to lift just one large one but could not. Finally he managed to pick up the smallest apple in sight, staggering with its weight, setting "out on his *via dolorosa* to the bus, carrying his torture."[5]

How accurately Lewis describes Ikey's (and our) avarice: "carrying his torture"! Then a "great voice" ordered Ikey to give up his gold collecting. The "thunderous yet liquid voice" came from a nearby waterfall.

Disregarding the angel's call to lay it down, to turn and take delight in the *real* apples of paradise, Ikey staggered, burdened with his loot, struggling to return to hell, where he vainly imagined that gold matters.

"Deathwater"

Lewis makes a similar point in *The Voyage of "The Dawn Treader."* A party of the adventurers was looking for the missing "seven lords" of Narnia. They explored an island and found a "deep little mountain lake," with some Narnian artifacts—a helmet and some coins—nearby. Then they saw at the bottom of the lake "a life-size figure of a man, made apparently of gold."[6] The little mouse, Reepicheep, suggested they dive into the waters and salvage the statue. But Edmund decided to first test the water's depth with his spear. When he tried to pull out the spear, it slipped from his hands and sank. Then he noticed the toes of his boots, which had touched the water, had turned to gold! The party realized that the water had exerted its magic, that the missing lord had removed his armor and dived into the lake, not suspecting its deadly power to turn people to gold.

The leader of the expedition, King Caspian, claimed the island for Narnia, naming it "Goldwater Island." He envisioned the power such unlimited wealth would bring and swore everyone to secrecy. Almost immediately the company divided, and Edmund and Caspian nearly crossed swords. At that moment, they saw "the hugest Lion that human eyes have ever seen."[7] He didn't say a word, but his presence brought them all to their senses. Then Reepicheep, ever courtly, declared the place accursed. Indeed, he said, "If I might have the honour of naming this island, I should call it Deathwater".[8]

Not Goldwater, but Deathwater! That's the difference avarice makes! It turns the life-giving goodness of earth into a lifeless tomb.

"A Tenant of the Spirit of the Age"

Today's world celebrates an unabashed "consumer" culture and follows the message of plushly positioned worldlings such as the "Clevers" in *The Pilgrim's Regress*. Our neighbors, like the Clevers, are enslaved by Mammon, who "is a tenant of the Spirit of the Age: who holds directly of the enemy."[9] That enemy is brilliantly exposed in Lewis's *Screwtape Letters,* when Screwtape instructs his nephew Wormwood to appeal to his subject's "sense of ownership," a claim that sounded "equally funny in Heaven and in Hell," but taken seriously by earthlings.[10]

When we reduce everything—from my coat to my parents to my nation—to the "my" of ownership, we become illiberal, as Aristotle made clear, drawing an important distinction between prodigality and illiberality. Prodigals covet riches to waste them on sensual pleasures. Illiberal folks, evident in misers like Silas Marner, delight to simply acquire riches they never use. The good person, Aristotle taught, is financially *liberal*—giving the right amounts to the right people at the right time.

Neither Aristotle, nor his saintly interpreter, Thomas Aquinas, condemned a healthy desire for financial comfort or legitimate gain. It's healthy, for example, to desire a house—a place to make a home. For most of us, our family is our most important earthly society, and we need a secure setting for it. As Thomas Aquinas insisted, it's fine for a man to seek, "according to a certain measure, to have external riches, in so far as they are necessary for him to live in keeping with his condition of life."[11]

In his autobiography, *Surprised by Joy,* Lewis expresses how he loved the large, rambling house his well-to-do lawyer father built on the outskirts of Belfast. "The 'New House,' as we continued for years to call it, was a large one even by my present standards; to a child it seemed less like a house than a city." Though it was, rather like his father, structurally flawed, "none of this . . . mattered to a child. To me, the important thing about the move [to the New House] was that the background of my life became larger. The New House is almost a major character in my story."[12]

We, like Lewis, need homes to live well. Homeless people suffer. Something is simply wrong about being homeless, even when you're homeless by choice. And we're right to want to secure and protect our homes.

The good life, like a healthy houseplant, forever stands rooted in the loam of home. Wars like the American Revolution are fought, James Otis insisted, because "a man's house is his castle; and whilst he is quiet, he is well guarded as a prince in his castle." Although a house is not a home, it's difficult to have a home without a house. We're physical creatures, and we need physical structures to live in. We rightly want to build and beautify, to protect and preserve, a house.

My wife and I live in a San Diego townhouse that is adequate for our needs. Over the years my wife has papered and painted and redecorated, making this house a "home" with her signature etched all over it. It's ours, and we thank the Lord for it.

What's wrong with owning a home is the assumption that it's *absolutely mine*. At the heart of the temptation to covet is the assumption that we can *forever* own things. Rather than taking the bounties of earth as a gift from God and using them wisely, we're tempted to grasp and hoard and treasure our possessions.

"Cut Off from the Whole Human Race"

In *The Voyage of "The Dawn Treader,"* Eustace Scrubb complained about almost everything on the journey. He was a spoiled nine-year-old. When the adventurers were blown ashore on Dragon Island, Eustace slipped away to avoid work. He got lost and stumbled into a dragon's den, where he found a hoard of treasure.[13] "There were crowns . . . coins, rings, bracelets, ingots, cups, plates and gems."[14]

Imagining that the treasure would enable him to live royally, he calculated how to carry it away. He thought, "I wonder how much I can carry? That bracelet now—those things in it are probably diamonds—I'll slip that on my own wrist. Too big, but not if I push it right up here above my elbow."[15] Eustace then fell into a long sleep, filled with dragonish thoughts. When he awakened, he found himself transformed into a dragon.

And he felt pain in his arm, for a dragon's leg is much larger than a boy's arm. His precious "treasure" became a tourniquet, choking off the blood flow. He also knew he'd lost his true identity as a person, for when we love money, we lose the capacity to live humanely.

Later Eustace was delivered from his monster plight by Aslan. His dragon skin was painfully peeled away by Aslan's claws. The astringent water of a lake healed his wounds. The ache in his arm, caused by his desire for treasure, was eased, for when Aslan tossed him into the water, the pain eased away. In time he was a little boy again, dressed by Aslan, born again by the magic water. He carried none of the dragon's "treasure" out of the valley, but he became a better boy.

Security Shelters

We succumb to covetousness, in C. S. Lewis's opinion, primarily because we want to construct security shelters. We want to live free from dependency, especially any dependency on God.

The theme resounded throughout *Perelandra,* for the temptation the Green Lady faces is to seek "fixed land," where she need not acknowledge her created status. As Ransom pondered the new world, he understood one of life's prime principles. Though the "love of money is the root of all evil," the desire for security, to be exempt from reversals and misfortunes, explains money's allure.

Taking a different turn, in *The Abolition of Man,* Lewis noted that middle-class suburbia, even in the midst of World War II, relished comfort and security rather than eternal verities. "Man lives by bread alone," delivered by "the baker's van: peace matters more than honour and can be preserved by jeering at colonels and reading newspapers."[16]

Many of us pursue such security by incessant work. Obviously we need to work. That's part of being human. And it's fine to try to find the best job, the work that's right for us. It's fine to improve ourselves by working hard and getting better jobs. It's not covetous to want to do well, to advance in our vocation. But too often our work turns competitive, and we seek to outdo others. We may even maneuver to get the position, the office, the authority another person holds. We easily slip into the temptation to do anything to step inside what Lewis called the "Inner Ring," the circle of powerful persons who run an organization. Lewis said,

> **The quest of the Inner Ring will break your hearts unless you break it. But if you break it, a surprising result will follow. If in your working hours you make the work your end, you will presently find yourself all unawares inside the only circle in your profession that really matters. You will be one of the sound craftsmen, and other sound craftsmen will know it.**[17]

I've spent my life as a college professor. It's fine for me to want to do my best, to move up the ranks. I've moved from being an instructor to an assistant professor, then to being an associate professor, and finally to being a full professor, with its associated salary. But if I thought my department chairman has more influence and authority than I have and I wanted that position simply to increase my wages or gain preeminence, I would be coveting. If I wanted to take the place of my university's provost, I would be coveting. If I wanted to become president of the university and concocted schemes to dislodge the incumbent, I would be covetous.

As Paul testified, "I have learned in whatever state I am, to be content" (Phil. 4:11, NKJV). Our desire for prosperity must be restrained, for it plants an outpost of the world within our hearts. We prosper and are promoted; we become well-known and influential. We find ourselves so at home in the world that we forget our eternal home.

Yet many of us go through life, aching because of the constrictions of our possessions. Too many of us, collecting coins that carry the inscription "In God We Trust," fail to remember its tacit message: only God, not money, deserves our trust. Instead, we pursue elusive goals: "financial success," "economic security," "the good life," "having it all"—polite euphemisms for greed. Many of us, seekers of "the American dream," easily embrace Mark Twain's corruption of a familiar scripture: "It's not the love of money that's the root of all evil—it's the lack of money that's the root of all evil!" Still more, in his *Revised Catechism*, Twain wrote, "What is the chief end of man?—to get rich. In what way?—dishonestly if we can; honestly if we must. Who is God, the one and only true? Money is God. Gold and Greenbacks and Stock—father, son, and ghosts of same, three persons in one; these are the true and only God, mighty and supreme."[18]

Like an enormous electromagnet, money tugs at a shrapnel of metal each of us carries in our hearts. Its pervasive power indwells popular expressions: "Another day, another dollar"—indicating money gives meaning to the day. "You get what you pay for"—suggesting the worth of goods and services can be reduced to dollars and cents. "The almighty dollar"—indicating it is omnipotent. "Money talks"—most of us agree with Richard Armour, who said, "That money talks I'll not deny; / I heard it once—it said good-bye!"

Our heroes make lots of money. Athletes make millions a year for playing their sports. Entertainers collect fortunes for performing. Heavyweight boxers get millions for pounding opponents for a few minutes. Even the guys who get pounded get millions for their pain! We easily assume the importance of money, its almost sacred quality, because we live in a world that has been structured by the notion that one's worth lies in the abundance of possessions.

However, when we read the Bible, we find some things rarely change. As sinful men, avarice and greed forever remain our gods. Gluttons may want too much food, but they usually reach a limit of consumption. But there's no limit to the amount of money we can deposit in the bank. So money looks infinitely desirable. Just a bit more. We're drawn to it. We're deceived into thinking a little more money will finally fulfill us and make us what we long to be: happy.

The love of money separates us from God, displacing Him as the focus of our love. Far from God, we fail to find happiness, for real happiness comes only when we're rightly related to Him. Money damns us, not because it's intrinsically evil, but because it diverts us from our true vocation in life, serving God. So money, C. S. Lewis observed, threatens our sanctity. Greed and holiness can't bed down together. Misers are never saints—and saints are never misers. And that's why avarice, covetousness, is a deadly sin. So in short, "You shall not covet" (Exod. 20:17).

⌇ PART TWO ⌇

THE SEVEN CHRISTIAN VIRTUES

8 ✒ Prudence

"No 'Intellectual Slackers' Allowed"

God is no fonder of intellectual slackers than of any other slackers.[1]

ON THE BACK OF MY OFFICE DOOR is a poster of one of my heroes, Sitting Bull—the famed Hunkpapa Sioux chief. His visage presides over this statement: "Let us put our heads together and find what kind of a future we can make for our children." He knew, a century ago, what Ravi Zacharias, one of today's greatest Christian thinkers, insists: "The ultimate test of any civilization is what we do with our children."[2]

Increasing numbers of us fear we've done poorly with our children during the past several decades. It's evident in the twisted behavioral traits that mark too many of our youngsters. Murderous rampages of high school students remind us of a barbarism engulfing our children. Underlying such behavioral problems, William Bennett says, is something more profound than economic poverty or poor public schools. It's a moral poverty that comes from growing up "without loving, capable, responsible adults who teach you right from wrong."[3]

Poverty in America may be more onerous in daycare centers and in plush suburban homes, with their latchkey kids, than in the lives of "street people," who seem poorer!

So we need to find the right road. To teach our children how to live, we must know what is right and wrong. We generally appeal to "conscience" when making moral decisions. But what is conscience? Basically it fuses an inner compulsion to *do* what's right with an understanding of what we think *is* right. In the first sense, we must always obey our conscience and try to do what's right. But we must also discern precisely what is, in fact, right. Thus, we must learn to think, to reason rightly.

Right Reason Reigns:
Making Judgments

Early in *The Lion, the Witch, and the Wardrobe*, one of the children, Susan, skeptically doubted Lucy's account of the mysterious world she had entered through an old wardrobe. Responding to Susan's doubts, the professor who owned the house challenged her to think. To accuse someone of lying who was, in every other instance, quite honest, he said, is "a very serious thing; a very serious thing indeed."[4] When Susan wondered if, perhaps, Lucy might be mad, the Professor retorted that a glance at her revealed it. Susan wondered at his certainty, not accustomed to adult discourse.

"Logic!" said the Professor half to himself. "Why don't they teach logic at these schools? There are only three possibilities. Either your sister is telling lies, or she is mad, or she is telling the truth. You know she doesn't tell lies and it is obvious that she is not mad. For the moment then and unless any further evidence turns up, we must assume that she is telling the truth."[5]

Logic! Right reason! Weighing the evidence and acting in accord with the truth! Such, Lewis thought, informs moral activity.

In *The Pilgrim's Regress,* Lewis depicts his young protagonist, John, following many roads before getting on the right one. Early in the story, John is imprisoned by "Mr. Enlightenment," sitting in a "black hole," surrounded by prisoners afflicted with "Parrot Disease." In an illuminating moment, he suddenly realizes that his jailer is "talking nonsense,"[6] actually claiming that a cow's secretions—whether milk or manure—were all the same, providing we choose to define them as such. Incensed at the illogic of this talk, John challenged, "Are you a liar or only a fool, that you see no difference between that which Nature casts out as refuse and that which she stores up as food?"[7]

To those who assert that we "project" our ideas upon the world and shape it to our designs, Lewis always retorted that the world is what it is, not what we would like it to be! Ultimately John will be freed by reason, the divine gift that enables us to grasp the truth, to realize that our thinking is not confined to cultural limitations or shaped by traditional biases. What John needed throughout his journey was *prudence,* the practical wisdom that prescribes proper behavior.

This wisdom flourishes in what Aristotle and Thomas Aquinas called the *rational soul*, which was often called "reason." Lewis cited Chaucer's Parson, who said, "God should have lordship over reason, and reason over sensuality, and sensuality over the body of man."[8] Created "by the immediate act of God," this rational soul can discern divine truths in two ways: *intellectus* and *ratio. "Intellectus,"* Lewis says, "is that in man which approximates most nearly to angelic *intelligentia,"* the ability to immediately, intuitively grasp a truth. *Ratio,* on the other hand, is the process of reasoning from one truth to another. Anglican theologian Richard Hooker said, "Reason is the director of man's will, discovering in action what is good."[9] So reason, not feeling, should guide moral actions.

As Lewis notes, "Nearly all moralists before the eighteenth century regarded Reason as the organ of morality."[10] This was because "nearly all of them believed the fundamental moral maxims were intellectually grasped."[11]

"The belief that to recognize a duty was to perceive a truth— not because you had a good heart but because you were an intellectual being—had roots in antiquity." Plato and Aristotle, the Stoics, and Paul all celebrated right reason as the guide to good behavior. When Paul said even the Gentiles have a law "written in their hearts," he endorsed a Stoic conception of the natural law, "and would for centuries be so understood. Nor, during those centuries, would the word "hearts" have merely emotional associations.

"The Hebrew word which St. Paul represents by *kardia* would be more nearly translated 'Mind'; and in Latin, one who is *cordatus* is not a man of feeling but a man of sense."[12]

Without such reason we're morally lost.[13] If, for example, "the feeling of certainty which we express by words like *must be*" is nothing more than "a feeling in our own minds and not a genuine insight into realities beyond them—if it merely represents the way our minds happen to work—then we can have no knowledge."[14] We would be left without moral guidance. Lewis insisted that "the primary moral principles on which all others depend are rationally perceived. We 'just see' that there is no reason why my neighbour's happiness should be sacrificed to my own, as we 'just see' that things which are equal to the same thing are equal to one another."[15] "It is because all morality is based on such self-evident principles that we say to a man, when we would recall him to right conduct, 'Be reasonable.'"[16]

The Virtue of Prudence

When we're reasonable, we have prudence, the ability to see the truth and act rightly. Aristotle's definition—*recta ratio agibilium,* "right reason enacted"—details the essence of prudence: mentally preparing to act. When we wonder precisely what we should be, the "virtue tradition" has a well-reasoned response: *Bonum hominis est secundum rationem esse,* or "The good of man is to be in accord with reason." To reason right, to understand the structure and texture of reality, and to live according to that understanding, is to live right. As Augustine said, "Prudence is the knowledge of what to seek and what to avoid."[17]

Prudence is the preeminent virtue. Without it—without knowing the *truth* underlying *goodness*—ethical endeavors falter. The intellectual structure constructed by Thomas Aquinas declares that "Being precedes Truth, and that Truth precedes the Good."[18] To do good we must first see truth, knowing what it is that *is* good. So "Prudence is the '*measure*' of justice, of fortitude, of temperance."[19] A prudent person humbly opens his or her mind to the truth of God disclosed in all that's real.

The "virtue tradition" was, in many ways, definitively set forth by Aristotle, who believed it was rooted in human nature. What he called "prudence" is practical wisdom, the knowledge of how we should act in accord with our true nature "with regard to things that are good or bad for man."[20] To act right, we must choose—and to choose we must understand what is *good*. Morally good people are prudent, for they know *how* to be good. "Such a life will be too high for human attainment," Aristotle said, "but we ought, so far as in us lies, to put on immortality, and do all that we can to live in conformity with the highest that is in us; for even if it is small in bulk, in power and preciousness it far excels all the rest. Indeed it would seem that this is the true self of the individual."²¹ It's what we might call "truth to act by." It's practical wisdom, carefully thinking about why one acts and.where such acts will lead one.

God-Rooted

To know what's really good is to know, ultimately, the God who is real. Holy living must be rooted in holy thinking, the kind of philosophy that intricately interlaces, like the steel girders in a skyscraper, the classical Christian mind. Holiness loves what's *good* as revealed in what's *true* and seeks to enact it. The holy life is evident in what we *do,* living out Jesus' synopsis of the Law: loving God and others.

Loving God involves loving Him with *all* our *minds.* A sound holiness ethic fuses a warm heart with a clear head. Real love cultivates and implements wisdom.

Countering those modern thinkers who seem more anxious to *disclaim* than to *claim* certainty, Christian philosophers insist that whatever has *being* is knowable. So let's look in Lewis's works for the three elements of what Josef Pieper, following Thomas Aquinas, calls the "silent contemplation of reality": (1) *memoria,* (2) *docilitas,* and (3) *solertia.*

Memoria

Basic to Prudence is *memoria,* the accurate remembering of what's essential in ethical actions. Aquinas, Josef Pieper says, "adduces true-to-being memory as the first prerequisite for the perfection of prudence; and indeed this factor is the most imperiled of all."²² The fifth volume of the Narnian stories, *The Silver Chair,* records Jill's and Eustace's adventures as they seek the lost Prince of Narnia, Rilian. At the book's beginning, Aslan tells Jill how the children are to proceed, instructing her to remember four essential signs. They miss the first sign when Eustace fails to recognize and greet his old friend Caspian, who is now much older than he was when they first met in *The Voyage of "The Dawn Treader."*

Later, they do remember the fourth sign, cutting Prince Rilian's bonds in the underground chamber, thanks to the Marsh-wiggle Puddleglum's insistence that, however risky it seemed, they must follow the sign: "You see, Aslan didn't tell Pole what would happen. He only told her what to do." Whatever happens "that doesn't let us off following the Sign."[23]

Memory, of course, enables us to preserve the past. One of Satan's strategies is to rivet our attention on dreamworlds rather than real worlds, to despise what actually is and to hunger for what might be. In our bent toward sinning, we easily despise outdated things.

Screwtape instructs Wormwood to tempt his human subjects, to "work on their horror of the Same Old Thing"[24] to get them to stop asking, "Is it righteous? Is it prudent? Is it possible?"

Rather, we're to wonder about unanswerable questions such as, "Is it consistent with the general movement of our time? Is it progressive or reactionary? Is this the way history is going?" Satan's emissaries know "while their minds are buzzing in this vacuum, we have the better chance to slip in and bend them to the action *we* have decided on."[25] When we forget the lessons of the past, mapping life's course in accord with our desires for the future, we inevitably stray.

To counter Satan's attacks, nothing better serves us than good history. Modern people, Screwtape noted, rarely read history, and "only the learned read old books" and even they seem to learn little from it.[26] Scholars find interesting those views of past thinkers but discard them simply because they are old, so they "are now as little nourished by the past as the most ignorant mechanic who holds that 'history is bunk.'"[27]

Conversely, prudence comes when we carefully study the best men and women have thought and written. To immerse ourselves in the Scriptures, in the thought of Plato and Aristotle, or Augustine and Aquinas, opens the mind's gates. The old way of teaching, stressing moral virtues, brought boys to manhood. The loss of classical education, with its root in "prudence," has impaired modern humanity. Lewis wrote *The Pilgrim's Regress,* his earliest publication as a Christian, as a lament for "the decay of our old classical learning."[28]

In the Western tradition that nourished Lewis, intellects recognized the role of prudence in the virtuous life. The consensus held that "Being precedes Truth, and . . . Truth precedes the

Good. Indeed the living fire at the heart of the dictum is the central mystery of Christian theology: that the Father begets the Eternal Word, and that the Holy Spirit proceeds out of the Father and the Word."[29]

We can discern the truth that illuminates being. Despite our sinfulness and finitude, something of the original good implanted in our minds by God remains. What makes us truly human, Thomas Aquinas insisted, summarizing the meaning of "prudence," is that all our acts shall be informed by "reason perfected in the cognition of truth." Truth and reality are disclosed to those who have ears to hear, to those who, as Jesus said, have good eyes, to those who see things as they are.

Docilitas

To *memoria* add *docilitas*. Prudent persons are open-minded, anxious to understand the Truth, willing to obey what Truth requires. One's heart implements the convictions of his or her head. Prudent people want to discover truth rather than construct theories that soothe their consciences. Like Mary sitting at Jesus' feet—and unlike Martha bustling about doing practical things—thoughtful people cultivate attentive silences.

This is the nature of contemplative thought. A person might almost say that false philosophers, like "talking heads" on television, stress *communicating* while true philosophers stress *contemplating*.

The Greek word *theoria* was translated into Latin as *contemplatio,* from which comes the English word "contemplation." Rightly understood, Pieper says, contemplation "means a *loving* gaze, the beholding of the beloved."[30] Consequently, "For the true philosopher . . . the challenge seems to be this: to acknowledge, before any consideration of specifics and without regard to usefulness, that reality is *good in itself*—all things, the world, 'being' as such; yes, all that exists, and existence itself."[31] This it is what Thomas Aquinas meant by "reason," which is a

"regard for and openness to reality," and "acceptance of reality." And "truth" is to him nothing other than the unveiling and revelation of reality, of both natural and supernatural reality. Reason "perfected in the cognition of truth" is therefore the receptivity of the human spirit, to which the revelation of reality, both natural and supernatural reality, has given substance.[32]

During John's journey in *The Pilgrim's Regress,* Mother Kirk informs him he must follow some rules if he is to find his beloved island. She warns that he will pass through a realm filled with poisonous food, so he must follow the rules and eat what's right if he survives.

As Lewis reminds us, we're designed by God and for God. He's our food and drink. He sustains our very being with His Being.

In *That Hideous Strength,* we find two rival communities locked in mortal combat. The technicians at N.I.C.E. seek to bulldoze all vegetation to transform the created world. For the sake of "humanity," they're willing to indulge in propaganda and engage in any form of behavior, even murder. They represent in profound ways a totalitarian gnosticism, determined to remold the world in their own interests. The rival community, gathered around Ransom, the "Fisher-King" at St. Anne's (Anne is the mother of Mary), works and prays to preserve the good world as given us by God.

In her first encounter with the director (the Fisher-King), Jane pondered her obligation to "do what I think right." Responding to her concern, the director noted, "I am not allowed to be *too* prudent." He could never pretend that admirable ends justify ignoble means, for that was his enemies' strategy. There are "rules" given by "Masters," said Ransom.[33] To make the right choices, he says, they must discover the right rules.

Solertia

Third, prudence demands *solertia*—a clear-sighted, "perfected ability" to discern the difference between right and wrong. In *That Hideous Strength*, Jane Studdock proves valuable to the community of St. Anne's because she has been gifted with dreams that reveal truth concerning the great cosmic struggle. The director praised her for her "service." Evil principalities and powers had plotted "one of the most dangerous attacks ever made upon the human race," and her dreams revealed the N.I.C.E. corps at Belbury as the nerve center of it all.[34]

The director, Elwin Ransom, had appeared in the two preceding volumes of Lewis's space fictions, and he clearly represents prudence as the "perfected ability" to know what one should do. On Malacandra (portrayed in *Out of the Silent Planet*), he carefully listened to and learned from that planet's mysterious residents. On Perelandra (in *Perelandra*) he saw life as it really is and learned from the Green Lady and her Lord Maleldil. He learned the laws of the cosmos, principles embedded in the natural law.

To understand the "Natural Law," which must uphold moral standards, we must learn to discern the reality undergirding it. From the beginning of the human story, we have, like sailors testing the depth of the ocean floor, sought to fathom the reality behind the passing phenomenon of the material world. Theists believe that this reality is a cosmic mind, an awesome Intelligence whose ways are partially knowable to us, for we have minds.

In *The Abolition of Man,* Lewis labeled this Ultimate Source or Natural Law or Traditional Morality "the *Tao."* It's the soil for the roots of ethical standards, and without it the leaves dry up and the branches fall, making a wasteland without moral life. Since the Tao is as eternal as God himself, no "new" moral truths will appear. We can no more manufacture moral codes than we can eliminate war by "visualizing" peace.

To Lewis, "The rational and moral element in each human mind is a point of force from the Supernatural working its way into Nature, exploiting at each point those conditions which Nature offers, repulsed where the conditions are hopeless and impeded when they are unfavourable."[35]

The need for such divinely grounded "prudence" appears in a recent work by Yale Law School professor Stephen Carter, *Civility: Manners, Morals, and the Etiquette of Democracy.* In "Coda: The Civility of Silence," he says we're too busy, too addicted to clocks and calendars, too immersed in noise, to discern ultimate truths. Tragically, "if we lose the vast silences that help define the sounds that fall between them, we may lose the ability to appreciate the transcendent."

Deafened by our own sounds, we easily imagine we're the source of all that is. "The quiet spaces help to remind us of who and whose we truly are. Lying on one's back in the deep of a silent night, gazing for an hour at a sky brilliant with sharp, white stars, it is difficult to resist the tug of God."[36] He alone can give us the guidance we need to rebuild civility, to save our civilization.

Through contemplation, knowing the truth about what is, we then act appropriately. To know the end we should pursue and to know the proper means to realizing that end demands prudence. As Jesus said, "He that doeth truth cometh to the light" (John 3:21, KJV).

Peter, following his Lord, urged his readers, "Prepare your minds for action" (1 Pet. 1:13). We will find no better admonition for prudence.

9 ✑ Justice

"The Old Name for Fairness"

Justice means equality for equals,
and inequality for unequals.[1]

THE LAST BATTLE, the final volume of Lewis's *The Chronicles of Narnia,* begins when Narnia's reigning king, Tirian, responded to a beachtree nymph: "'Justice, Lord King,' she cried. 'Come to our aid. Protect your people. They are felling us in Lantern Waste. Forty great trunks of my brothers and sisters are already on the ground.'"[2] Astounded by such an attack on his subjects, Tirian reacted strongly. "'What, Lady! Felling Lantern Waste? Murdering the talking trees?' cried the King leaping to his feet and drawing his sword. 'How dare they?'"[3]

Overwhelmed by anger, Tirian dashed to where the Calormenes were cutting down the trees. There, assisted by the unicorn Jewel, he killed two of the Calormenes who were harnessing and whipping some talking horses as well as chopping down the talking trees. Impassioned to defend the innocents, determined to deter the Calormene invasion, the king swung his sword mightily. Then, vastly outnumbered by the Calormenes, King Tirian fled for his life, riding Jewel to safety.

Unexpectedly, the king ordered Jewel to stop, and he dismounted to ponder his deed. "'Jewel,' said the King. 'We have done a dreadful deed.'"[4] When the unicorn protested that they were fully justified in killing the Calormenes, the king replied: "But to leap on them unawares—without defying them—while they were unarmed—faugh! We are two murderers, Jewel. I am dishonoured forever."[5] Conscience-driven, Tirian turned and prepared to surrender to the Calormenes, asking them to "bring me before Aslan. Let him do justice to me."[6]

Rendering What's Due

With Tirian we know, in the depths of our being, that few issues outweigh the importance of justice. In one of Plato's dialogues, *Gorgias,* Socrates says a person should submit to anything—prison, pain, exile, even death—in order to "be freed from the greatest of evils, from injustice."[7] He thereby expressed one of our most deeply imbedded convictions, the Golden Rule's admonition to do to others as you would have them do to you. It's the basic premise of the natural law: do good, and don't do evil.

The first word many of us spoke was, "Mama." Then we said, "Dada." Then we put some words together and said, "That's not fair!" Few other charges echo so regularly around children's playgrounds. We're called to "play fair" with others, to sustain and spread righteousness. We're born with a little gyroscope that incessantly seeks to balance the scales of justice. As Lewis declared, justice is "fairness," keeping one's word, honest trade, fidelity to vows.

Following Socrates, the great thinkers of the Western tradition have often ranked justice as the highest of the moral virtues, primarily because it focuses on *others* and their well-being.[8] So, repeating Aristotle's definition,[9] Thomas Aquinas says, "Justice is a habit *(habitus)* whereby a man renders to each his due with constant and perpetual will."[10]

One Mark of a Good, Holy Person

In Holy Scripture the "good" or "holy" person is recognized as one who is "just," who upholds "justice" or "righteousness." The Ten Commandments teach us how to treat others. They are, in truth, "a comprehensive *Summa* of the whole field of moral thought."[11] In the Sermon on the Mount, Jesus said, "Seek ye first the kingdom of God, and his righteousness" (Matt. 6:33, KJV). Jerome translated the Greek word for righteousness (*dikaiosune*) as *justicia,* and the word "justice" is often used interchangeably with righteousness in Scripture. So to be holy, to do right, a person follows God's design by discerning and doing justice. An individual becomes what God designed him or her to be when he or she understands and does truth.

Such "justice" or "righteousness" aligns us with God and respects His handiwork. In *Out of the Silent Planet,* Elwin Ransom learned to respect the three species of creatures on Malacandra (Mars). Differently gifted, members of each of the species diligently followed their own designs, serving Oyarsa, the planet's Lord. They singularly sought to serve their Maker, but they also served each other. In many ways they illustrate Plato's longing for a "just society" in which various groups of people cooperate, much like parts of a body, for the common good. As Lewis makes clear, such cooperation is possible only where all groups obey a common Lord.

Reciprocal, Domestic Justice

This type of cooperation is evident in happy families, where peace and joy result from husbands and wives, parents and children, following their assigned roles. Aristotle calls this "domestic justice," and it's basic to good family life. Since justice "includes the keeping of promises,"[12] it requires that husbands and wives sustain their vows, recognizing they are "one flesh" and must live in accord with their Lord's instructions. Men and women have divinely assigned roles. Lewis says men deal best with the family's "foreign policy," seeking to deal fairly with outsiders. The woman, more likely to tenaciously fight for her children, serves as a "special trustee" for them. Each role is crucial. Each must be respected.

So Lewis begins his novel *That Hideous Strength,* "'Matrimony was ordained, thirdly,' said Jane Studdock to herself, 'for the mutual society, help, and comfort that the one ought to have of the other.' She had not been to church since her schooldays until she went there six months ago to be married, and the words of the service had stuck in her mind."[13] Jane's discontent stemmed from the fact that neither she nor her husband, Mark, had accepted the obligations of marriage. They had failed to live up to their vows, to treat each other justly.

When, as the story unfolds, she seeks solace in St. Anne's community, ultimately acknowledging the director's lordship, she also had to yield to her husband's headship in her marriage. In her initial interview with the director, Ransom told her to seek Mark's permission to join the community. She bristled at the suggestion, since she had held tenaciously to her own rights in marriage, retorting that she and the director probably differed as to marriage's ingredients. Love, she thought, entailed equality and personal freedom, but Ransom disabused her of such fantasies. In politics, in commerce, one might speak of equality, but it's not ultimately that important.

Leaving Ransom and St. Anne's, Jane pondered what she had felt in his presence. She had experienced an ethereal inner peace, an assurance that St. Anne's was the right place for her. She had encountered within herself an unexpected "moral Jane," formerly unknown to her. The voice of conscience reminded her of truths she'd heard about but never "connected with real life," the things she'd never before "connected with real life."[14] This inner voice aroused "new feelings about Mark, feelings of guilt and pity," first felt in the director's presence. She knew, deep in her heart, that he spoke truly. And, amazingly enough, her thoughts about Mark meshed with her feelings for Ransom, and she sensed her yielding to her husband would signify a submission to the director.[15]

Reciprocal, Punitive Justice

Personal righteousness—heart holiness—not only applies to the inner condition of a person's heart but also guides the social and political activities of his or her life as a citizen. In subtle ways, everything we do has social ramifications, whether we consciously design this or not, and we are called to sustain and spread justice. So we struggle to balance concern for personal and social morality.

Punishing lawbreakers has always been one of justice's primary concerns. A controversy agitating England during Lewis's era was capital punishment. Some "humanitarians" objected to it, insisting it was inhumane and barbaric. Responding in an essay, "The Humanitarian Theory of Punishment," Lewis argued that taking a murderer's life was more "just" than trying to rehabilitate him or her through therapeutic techniques. Under the "old view," sentencing a criminal implemented a moral understanding of reality; under the "new view," sentencing overlooks the crime and tries to restore the criminal. It sought to "abolish justice and substitute Mercy for it."[16] But "Mercy, detached from Justice, grows unmerciful."[17] Lewis feared such "Humanitarianism," for "of all tyrannies a tyranny sincerely exercised for the good of its victims may be the most oppressive. It may be better to live under robber barons than under omnipotent moral busybodies."[18] So he insisted that it is

> **essential to oppose the Humanitarian theory of punishment, root and branch, wherever we encounter it. It carries on its front a semblance of mercy which is wholly false. That is how it can deceive men of good will. The error began, perhaps, with Shelley's statement that the distinction between mercy and justice was invented in the courts of tyrants. . . . But the distinction is essential.[19]**

In one passage of *Mere Christianity*, C. S. Lewis aptly compared morality with ships in a convoy. Individual ships must be sound in order to sail. Yet they must sail on a sea dotted with other ships. Problems develop when folks go their separate ways, refusing to cooperate or running into each other, doing their own things. Morality includes treating others fairly, doing justice.[20]

Though love, for Christians, infuses all activities, "justice" guides our relationships with others who are basically "strangers" to us. Basic to the "love ethic" is the "Golden Rule," doing to others what we want them to do to us.

This means, strangely enough, that we may have to punish those we love. Augustine insisted in his commentary on 1 John, "Do not imagine that thou then lovest thy servant when thou doest not beat him, or that thou then lovest thy son when thou givest him not discipline, or that thou then lovest thy neighbor when thou doest not rebuke him. This is not charity, but mere feebleness."[21]

Lewis agreed. Loving our enemies does not exclude punishing evil doers. I can love myself and still approve of certain punishments when I do wrong. So soldiers who kill in war, judges who sentence criminals to prison, seek justice. As such, their acts do not exclude love.

The "Justice of Inequality"

Traditionally, justice meant *equity*, giving to each person what he or she deserved. More recently, influential thinkers such as Harvard University's John Rawls in *A Theory of Justice* have equated justice with *equality*. In a "just" world, they think, everyone would have the same amount of everything. Much about the modern liberalism, with its "welfare state," seeks to implement this philosophy. Though markedly nonpolitical in many ways, C. S. Lewis resisted such views and held a very traditional commitment to justice. His primary concern was for "reciprocal justice," doing right to those around us. He said, "Justice means equality for equals, and inequality for unequals."[22]

Significantly, "Equality is a quantitative term and therefore love often knows nothing of it. . . . Even in the life of the affections, much more in the body of Christ, we step outside that world which says 'I am as good as you.' . . . We become, as Chesterton said, taller when we bow; we become lowlier when we instruct."[23] He endorsed Plato's admonition that political leaders should remember that justice gives to everyone, in accord with his or her abilities, what is due him or her. Only in crises when political turmoil threatens did Plato note that "it is inevitable that equality—'so called' equality, as Plato terms it—take the place of justice."[24]

Taking Plato's perspective, resolutely defending the justice of "inequality," Lewis challenged one of modernity's most widely embraced notions of "justice," with its equalitarian rhetoric and utopian schemes. While some demands come from a "desire for fair play," which is admirable, many come from a "hatred for superiority," which is utterly misguided.[25] In fact *just* distinctions exist, which reflect real differences between humans. Not every student deserves an A on an exam. Not every athlete deserves a gold medal in the Olympics. Not every employee deserves the same salary. Any society offers legitimate ranks. "A just and legitimate society, according to Aristotle, is one in which inequalities—of property, or station, or power—are generally perceived by the citizenry as necessary for the common good."[26]

Distributive Justice: Life, Liberty, Property

It's important, when studying justice, when seeking to live

justly, that we rightly understand social and economic justice, and uphold the *justitia distributiva,* which "is the very center of the theory of justice."[27] In any society, some people are more powerful than others. Those with power, especially political power, have a responsibility to rightly distribute common goods—to protect everyone's life, to respect human freedom, to secure private property. All of us have a right to those common goods we share simply by virtue of being human. So those in positions of authority have a holy assignment, for "in the affairs of the world, everything depends on the rulers' being just."[28]

Throughout Lewis's Narnian chronicles, this truth reigns. The children who journey from earth to Narnia must demonstrate their courage and character before receiving ruling positions. As "kings" and "queens," they assume a sacred task: to distribute justice to their subjects. They're lauded for their goodness, their integrity. Thomas Aquinas declared that the just ruler will "as his reward, be near God and stand at His side inasmuch as he has faithfully exercised the king's divine office over his people."[29] Good rulers respect the rule of law that preserves the well-being of their subjects. Laws, rightly enforced, protect everyone. Evil regimes not only fail to protect, but actually deprive their subjects of such goods as life, liberty, and property.

Not "Entitlements"

We routinely hear of victims who demand their "rights" as demanded by "justice." This is evident in the many sentimental stories regarding victims whose rights have been compromised. In demanding rights, we appeal to justice, that ultimate standard of fairness. We live in a world in which people increasingly claim "entitlements" to get what they don't have by taking it from others. These desires seem to be rooted in what they see as their absolute rights. Yet, as Lewis noted,

> **If all men stood talking of their rights before they went up a mast or down a sewer or stoked a furnace or joined an army, we should all perish; nor while they talked of their rights would they learn to do these things. . . . The man preoccupied with his own rights is not only a disastrous, but a very unlovely object; indeed, one of the worst mischiefs we do by treating a man unjustly is that we force him to be thus preoccupied.[30]**

Justice certainly recognizes legitimate rights. To give a person what's due him or her, the person must obviously first possess certain rights. Traditionally, rights were understood as given to us by creation—what are called "unalienable" in the United States Declaration of Independence.

Rights come to us by virtue of our creation. God alone grants rights. Modern rights rhetoric, however, reflects a major shift in the West's moral tradition—a turning from the Christian understanding of humanity as innately sinful to a humanistic belief in the essential goodness of humanity. An acknowledged sinner certainly confesses his or her needs and asks for help, acknowledging that his or her rights are God-given. But a humanist demands entitlements, arguing that he or she has been victimized by his or her environment, imprisoned by wrongs done to his or her ethnic group, oppressed by sexism or age or whatever!

Justice has come to mean getting what a person wants, not what is truly due him or her.

Nor "Redistributive Social Justice"

As a result, social justice has become a concern for many people. The list of entitlements due to a person simply because he or she is a member of some group has expanded during the past decades. In any society, from the family to the state, equity in economic issues proves crucial. Especially unjust to many—such as Marx—is the inequality of wealth, which characterizes capitalistic economies, largely the consequence of the industrial revolution. So social justice advocates cry for the redistribution of wealth.

In redistributing wealth, the state becomes increasingly powerful. To Lewis, this growth was alarming. The power that it has assumed, Lewis suggests (in works such as *The Abolition of Man* and *That Hideous Strength*), threatens to overwhelm individuals, families, voluntary communities. In one letter he wrote, "We hear too much of the State. Government is at its best a necessary evil."[31] And when it becomes totalitarian, it's *totally* evil!

One person who knows the nature of totalitarianism is Balint Vazsonyi, a concert pianist who fled his native Hungary after freedom fighters failed to dislodge their Soviet oppressors in 1956. He sought and found in the United States a remarkably free, open, vibrant country that he enthusiastically embraced and made his own. He actually felt as if he had landed on a different planet, so dramatically better were things here than in Communist Europe. And he particularly fell in love with the United States Constitution and the rule of law it secures for all citizens.

But times have changed, and in *America's 30 Years War: Who Is Winning?* Vazsonyi articulates his growing concerns for his adopted land.[32] Having watched the Nazis impose their regime in Budapest in 1944 and then the Soviets theirs in 1948, he knows that they both espoused equally brutal variants of totalitarianism.

He especially learned to understand how much "social justice" rhetoric subtly enshrouds plans for totalitarian socialism— for the "good" of the many an enlightened few seize control of a state and stay in control to pursue their own interests. Thus, a decade after arriving in the United States, he watched in amazement as his finest music students began to repeat clichés he had heard in Hungary two decades earlier. They sang softly of love and peace, but their speech resonated with the code words and phrases he had heard during the Nazi and Soviet occupations.[33]

Justification for departing from the United States' most tested traditions stemmed from a naive commitment to "social justice," which Vazsonyi believes to be "among the most successful deceptions ever conceived."[34]

"The essence of communism is social justice—the elimination of poverty, the elimination of suffering, the elimination of all differences that erect walls between people."[35] Although few people in the United States openly embrace the label "communist" or "socialist," we are urged to pursue "universal health care" and the "redistribution of wealth," to expect the state to care for the impoverished, to impose "speech codes, sensitivity training, restrictions on parents' rights, school-to-work—the list goes on and on. The agenda is with us, the Party is not."[36] However alluring, Vazsonyi believes, all such goals propose various injustices under the rubric of "social justice."

To all such issues, we must bring a concern for justice, rightly defined and defended. As Micah insisted, "He hath shewed thee, O man, what is good; and what doth the LORD require of thee, but to do justly, and to love mercy, and to walk humbly with thy God?" (Mic. 6:8, KJV).

10 ✍ Courage

"The Form of Every Virtue"

*Fortitude includes both kinds of courage—
the kind that faces danger as well as the kind
that "sticks it" under pain. "Guts" is perhaps
the nearest modern English.*[1]

LEGENDARY GREEN BAY PACKERS COACH Vince Lombardi once said, "If you're lucky enough to find a guy with a lot of smarts and a lot of heart, he'll always come off the field first." Whether intentionally or not, Lombardi highlighted two classic cardinal virtues—prudence (smarts) and courage (heart). Failing to combine the two means that too often those who know what to do fail to do so, and those who have the courage to act often act wrong! But prudence (practical wisdom) and fortitude (the "guts" to do what's wise) combine in virtuous persons. Today, as always, courage counts.

Defying Death, Disarming Discouragement

Fortitude frees a person from inordinate fear of death. A courageous soldier neither flees in battle nor takes foolish risks. The courageous person risks his or her life when the cause is just. "It is for the sake of the good," said Thomas Aquinas, "that the brave man exposes himself to the danger of death."[2] As with the other virtues, the external act, not the internal feelings, count. As Screwtape said, "Remember: the *act* of cowardice is all that matters; the emotion of fear is, in itself, no sin and, though we enjoy it, does us no good."[3]

Though we often illustrate this virtue in military heroes, Aquinas insists mundane, daily "endurance is more of the essence of fortitude than attack."[4] To patiently endure, to stand firm amid criticism and adversity, reveals true courage. To rear children, to work faithfully, to pastor a congregation may easily demand more fortitude than momentary heroics that lead to martyrdom. Ruth Graham said that as a young girl she sometimes fantasized about dying as a missionary martyr. Now in her 80s, however, she's coming to terms with the "martyrdom of old age," something that is surely just as trying. So the demonic Screwtape counsels Wormwood to try to keep his young Christian alive, for comfort and prosperity would make it harder for him to persevere in his Christian faith. The dissipating dreams and hollowed-out hopes, the growing despair of old age —all provide time and chance to dry out "a soul by attrition."[5]

Cowardice Amply Evident

Whether or not courage counts today seems debatable. We live in what some have termed the era of the antihero. Victims, rather than the victors, often gain our attention and applause. A 1995 issue of *Newsweek* featured an essay on children's books titled "Underdog Days." Kids are now being spoon-fed stories of "a timid bear. A failing math student. A chicken on the run. Kids' books pay homage to the antihero." For instance, Edward the Unready is a perpetually worried little bear whose parents seem determined to soothe his every frustration with cinnamon toast, hugs, and kisses. Banished forever, it seems, from children's literature are kids who take responsibility, struggle to achieve, fall down, and get up and push on.

This absence of courage and abolition of heroes is a sign of the times. Aleksandr Solzhenitsyn has written,

A decline in courage may be the most striking feature that an outside observer notices in the West today. The Western world has lost its civic courage, both as a whole and separately, in each country, in each government, in each political party, and, of course, in the United Nations. Such a decline in courage is particularly noticeable among the ruling and intellectual elites, causing an impression of a loss of courage by the entire society.[6]

In a prophetic passage in *The Abolition of Man*, Lewis anticipated Solzhenitsyn's lament, explaining that syllogisms never
sustain soldiers when called to battle. Irrational feelings for flags
or battalions or sweethearts back home provide a stronger im-
petus. We long for heroism. Yet much modern education, including recent removal from public schools of plaques portraying the Ten Commandments, crushes the spirit, leaving "men
without chests." Heads fill up with information, but hearts atrophy. "In a sort of ghastly simplicity we remove the organ and
demand the function. We make men without chests and expect
of them virtue and enterprise. We laugh at honour and are
shocked to find traitors in our midst. We castrate and bid the
geldings be fruitful."[7]

And yet we know it's wrong! In our hearts we know, as
Shakespeare's Julius Caesar said, "Cowards die many times before their deaths; the valiant taste of death but once."[8] And in
our dreams, we still long to be courageous, to be heroes. So
people flock to movies such as *Patriot* and *Saving Private Ryan,*
which at least celebrate the grandeur of people who fight and
die for what they believe.

Battlefield Illustrations

Such battle was graphically portrayed by Lewis in *Perelandra*.
Elwin Ransom is sent to Venus to save the planet from the powers of evil, present in the monomaniacal Weston (the "Un-
man"), who seeks to seduce the Green Lady. Upon his arrival,
Ransom engages Weston in lengthy debates, championing the
cause of righteousness. But ultimately it becomes evident that
mere words will not win the battle.

Struggling with Weston's wiles, Ransom wondered why
Maleldil (the Lord) did not miraculously intervene. Yet in the
darkness he knew that Maleldil was there as surely as a magnetic pole pulling on a compass. Ransom was immersed in a divine Presence standing on holy ground. His inner debate waned
when he realized he was on Perelandra by providential order.
There was a reason for him to be there, and his presence was
the "miracle" needed to do God's work.

His efforts at first seemed inept, like a child struggling to
lace his or her shoes. But an overwhelming certainty dawned.

His presence on Perelandra "was not a moral exercise, nor a sham fight." The planet's future depended on him. He must fight, for everything hinged on it.[9]

The issue, it seemed to him, rivaled that of Horatius, defending the bridge in ancient Rome—or Constantine embracing the Christian faith and committing his imperial forces to defending it. Nothing less *physical* was required of Ransom. And the fate of the planet rested on his shoulders. "'It is not for nothing that you are named Ransom,' said the Voice."[10] Still he struggled, trembling at the task. Yet he remembered twice before—once in the war and once again when confessing an embarrassing failure—he'd done the "impossible." Once again he must rise to the challenge.

And he did. He resolved, though untrained, to engage Weston in combat—to kill the "Un-man." Once the fight began, he was surprised at his own strength, for he had assumed that he would quickly die trying to destroy his enemy. Standing firm in battle filled "Ransom not with horror but with a kind of joy."[11]

The "joy" he felt derived from the courage (the brave-heartedness) that marks a truly good man or woman. Sir Winston Churchill once declared that "without courage, all the other virtues lose their value." C. S. Lewis makes the same point in *The Screwtape Letters*, warning that, ironically, if a man acts cowardly he will probably feel conviction for failing to be a man. Then he might repent and let God transform him into a man of substance. So Screwtape instructed Wormwood, God (the Enemy) probably made the world filled with dangers and trials so as to elicit courage in human hearts. From His standpoint, "Courage is not simply *one* of the virtues, but the form of every virtue at the testing point, which means, at the point of highest reality."[12]

As cowardice opens us to temptation, so courage is "the form of every virtue" that enables us to act well, to be holy. Though some vices (such as greed) may have advocates, we rarely hear cowardice praised—except in such 1960s slogans as "better red than dead." Yet, as Thomas Aquinas insisted, "It is for the sake of the good that the brave man exposes himself to the danger of death."[13]

All too often holiness has been equated with spineless behavior. Holy people are imagined to be like an imaginary "gentle Jesus, meek and mild" who never offends, never stands up to evil persons. Rather, as Lewis quotes Cicero, "Nature and reason command that nothing uncomely, nothing effeminate, nothing lascivious be done or thought."[14] Those who equate sanctity with softness generally misunderstand Jesus' command to "turn the other cheek" when struck by an enemy.

In his commentary on John's Gospel, Thomas Aquinas, following Augustine, said we must interpret Jesus' words "in the light of what Christ and the saints have actually practiced. Christ did not always offer His other cheek, nor Paul either."

Taking the words "turn the other cheek" too literally leads us astray. Jesus meant we should readily "bear, *if it be necessary,* such things and worse, without bitterness against the attacker." We should have the courage, as Jesus modeled, "to be crucified" if God wills it.[15] To "turn the other cheek" does not, however, mean to avoid combat, to flee from the evil foes, to turn away when they harm innocent people.

In Lewis's works, courage characterizes many of his most righteous characters. His love for medieval life and literature included a profound love for the ethos of chivalry. One of his essays, "The Necessity of Chivalry," praises the fabled knight Lancelot, who, in Malory's *Le Morte d'Arthur,* is described, as "the meekest man that ever ate in hall among ladies; and thou wert the sternest knight to thy mortal foe that ever put spear in the rest."[16]

As Lewis noted, this courtly ideal made a "double demand" on its followers. In battle, a chivalrous knight is rugged and fearless, ready to ravage foes, willing to face death without fleeing from combat.

Taking a stand, doing what's right, typically exposes one to a kind of death, so "all fortitude has reference to death."[17] The ultimate Christian courage, of course, is martyrdom—bearing witness to one's faith and love by dying. "Thomas Aquinas seems to consider it to be almost the nature of fortitude that it fights against the *superior* power of evil, which the brave man can defeat only by his death or injury."[18] But away from the roar of battle—and especially in the presence of ladies—the knight is retiring, modest, merciful. He is, Lewis said, "fierce to the nth and meek to the nth."[19] Thus, courageous men are at times wrathful.

Thomas Aquinas says, "The brave man uses wrath for his own act, above all in attack, 'for it is peculiar to wrath to pounce upon evil. Thus fortitude and wrath work directly upon each other.'"[20]

Training Knights

Brave men, courtly knights, Lewis thought, are needed in the modern world. "If we cannot produce Lancelots," Lewis thought, "humanity falls into two sections—those who can deal in blood and iron but cannot be 'meek in hall,' and those who are 'meek in hall' but useless in battle."[21] The integrity of "Lancelot" is never outdated, so each generation must educate modern Lancelots to assume their two-dimensional calling.

This conviction led Lewis not only to praise medieval chivalry but also to inject its values into his stories, especially *The Chronicles of Narnia.* As King Tirian said to his followers in *The Last Battle,* "No warrior scolds. Courteous words or else hard knocks are his only language."[22] That gentlemanly ideal is evident in *Prince Caspian,* when the evil Miraz fell in the midst of a battle. Rather than strike him as he lay helpless, King Peter waited for him to rise and do battle. Evaluating Peter's chivalry, Edmund thought, "Oh bother, bother, bother." He wondered, "Need he be as gentlemanly as all that? I suppose he must. Comes of being a Knight *and* a High King. I suppose it is what Aslan would like."[23] And that *is* just what Aslan likes—men risking even death to *be* men of character.

The call to courage begins in *The Lion, the Witch, and the Wardrobe.* After Aslan delivered Narnia from the cold winter of the witch's control, he shows Peter the majestic Cair Paravel, a castle with four thrones, where Peter will preside as "High King" over Narnia. But first he must "win his spurs" in his "first battle," defending his sister Susan from a ferocious wolf.

> **Peter did not feel very brave; indeed, he felt he was going to be sick. But that made no difference to what he had to do. He rushed straight up to the monster and aimed a slash of his sword at its side. That stroke never reached the Wolf. Quick as lightning it turned round, its eyes flaming, and its mouth wide open in a howl of anger. . . . though all this happened too quickly for Peter to think at all—he had just time to duck**

down and plunge his sword, as hard as he could, between the brute's forelegs into its heart.[24]

The Wolf slain, Peter and his sister stood, shaking, on the field of battle. Then the lordly lion Aslan appeared. In a moving ceremony, Aslan took Peter's sword and "struck him with the flat of the blade and said, 'Rise up, Sir Peter Fenris-Bane.'"[25]

With this preparation, Peter led an army in a fierce struggle against the witch's forces and won the battle, delivering Narnia from her control.

In the next Narnian chronicle, *Prince Caspian,* a young prince is called to exert great courage in taking his rightful kingdom from his evil uncle. A loyal corps of "Old Narnians" are willing to undertake a "real war to drive Miraz out of Narnia."[26] Among the creatures was "the last thing Caspian expected—a Talking Mouse."[27] Readers then encounter one of Lewis's most delightful creatures: Reepicheep. Standing nearly a foot tall, "he was a gay and martial mouse. He wore a tiny little rapier at his side and twirled his long whiskers as if they were a moustache."[28]

In the struggles to come, Reepicheep always counseled courageous action. He personified chivalry and courage, sometimes bordering on rashness, but always ready to unsheathe his rapier for righteousness. In *Prince Caspian,* Reepicheep is seriously wounded in battle—even losing his beloved tail. With loving care, Aslan heals Reepicheep and restores his tail, praising the courage of the knightly mice and his comrades. "You have great hearts," he declared.[29]

In *The Voyage of "The Dawn Treader,"* Reepicheep—"a foot-and-a-half of courage"—again appears. Lewis noted that the book is about the "spiritual life (especially in Reepicheep)."[30] Now he is called the "Chief Mouse." Early in the ship's journey, the spoiled child, Eustace, insulted Reepicheep by twirling him by his tail. Reepicheep, veteran of many battles, calmly drew his sword, escaped from his tormentor, and charged, twirling his *rapier* uncomfortably close to Eustace's body.

When Eustace demanded that Reepicheep put away his sword, the mouse challenged him to a duel. Called to draw his sword, "'I haven't got one,' said Eustace. 'I'm a pacifist. I don't believe in fighting.'"[31] Astounded by such a response, Reepicheep resolved to teach the earthling a lesson, slapping him with the flat side of his sword, made of "fine dwarf-tempered steel and as supple and effective as a birch rod. Eustace (of course) was at a school where they didn't have corporal punishment, so the sensation was for him a complete novelty."[32]

When the *Dawn Treader* crew repeatedly faced unknown dangers, Reepicheep continually urged valor and courage in pressing ahead, battling evil, and refusing to flee darkness. In battles, he demonstrated his willingness to die. And at the end of the story, he boarded a little boat and sailed off the edge of the world, expecting to enter Aslan's eternal kingdom.

Churchill, Thatcher

Winston Churchill urged courage upon the students at Harrow School during World War II. He said, "Never give in, never give in, never, never, never, never—in nothing, great or small, large or petty—never give in except to convictions of honor and good sense."[33] That describes the courage that won the war, the courage to stand and fight the forces of evil.

Though we're not at war physically, we're always at war with the "principalities and powers of this world." So we must remember, as did Joshua, that our strength comes from the God who has promised to be with us. Ultimately, as Churchill said, "Success is never final. Failure is never fatal. It's courage that counts."

One of this century's finest statespeople, Margaret Thatcher, lived Churchill's maxim. Known as "the Iron Lady," she demonstrated courage that only comes from deep convictions. These convictions were established during her early years as she attended a Methodist church. In contrast to unprincipled politicians who waffle with the winds of popular opinion, Lady Thatcher refused to bend when principles such as freedom and justice were at stake. Responding to those who urged compromise and "consensus," she replied,

> To me consensus seems to be: The process of abandoning all beliefs, principles, values and policies in search of something in which no one believes, but to which no one objects; the process of avoiding the very issues that have to be solved, merely because you cannot get agreement on the way ahead. What great cause could have been fought and won under the banner "I stand for consensus"?[34]

Christians, like Thatcher, should stand not for consensus nor for a weak-kneed pluralism that declares "whatever." We stand for Christ and His Word. And this requires courage. In the final chapter of Joshua, the elderly leader addressed his people for the last time. He reminded them of how God had blessed the children of Abraham. Then he said,

Now therefore, fear the LORD, serve Him in sincerity and in truth, and put away the gods which your fathers served on the other side of the River and in Egypt. Serve the LORD! And if it seems evil to you to serve the LORD, choose for yourselves this day whom you will serve. . . . But as for me and my house, we will serve the LORD *(Josh. 24:14-15, NKJV).*

11 ✍ Temperance

"Going the Right Length"

The New Testament has lots to say about self-denial, but not about self-denial as an end in itself.[1]

GREEK HISTORIAN THUCYDIDES said we should not "believe that there is much difference between man and man, but to think that the superiority lies with him who is reared in the severest school."[2] On a lesser battlefield, the late Dallas Cowboys head coach Tom Landry said, "Most successful football players not only accept rules and limitations but, I believe, they need them. Players are free to perform at their best only when they know what the expectations are, where the limits stand."[3]

Good athletes exemplify a self-control that comes in part from following coaches' instructions. No matter how much people wish to excel in an activity, they need help to focus their thoughts and actions to attain their goals. On their own, the unsanctified generally follow their natural bent to sinning, which destroys them.

William Bennett says, "The good requires constant reinforcement and the bad needs only permission."[4] Self-discipline never deforms us. It frees us! Temperance enables athletes to stay in shape and compete in the game. To Lewis,

> Discipline, while the world is yet unfallen, exists for the sake of what seems its very opposite—for freedom, almost for extravagance. The pattern deep hidden in the dance, hidden so deep that shallow spectators cannot see it, alone gives beauty to the wild, free gestures that fill it, just as the decasyllabic norm gives

beauty to all the licenses and variations of the poet's verse. The happy soul is, like a planet, a *wandering star*; yet in that very wandering (as astronomy teaches) invariable; she is eccentric beyond all predicting, yet equable in her eccentricity.[5]

Defining the Virtue

Temperance (derived from the Latin word *temperare*—"to mix together in due proportions") helps us practice moderation and restraint. Temperance applies to all of life and rightly orders everything in its proper place. Augustine said, "The function of temperance is to control and quell the desires which draw us to the things which withdraw us from the laws of God and from the fruit of His goodness . . . it is the duty of temperance to spurn all bodily allurements and popular praise."[6] Legendary Athenian lawgiver Solon declared, "Nothing in excess." Lewis defined temperance as applying "to all pleasures; and it meant not abstaining, but going the right length and no further."[7]

Empowered by the Holy Spirit, holy people find the strength to healthily maintain their integrity through self-discipline. God has "tempered the body together" said Paul, meaning, as the original Greek word *sophrosyne* indicates, temperance has a "directing reason."

"Thus God," Paul continued, "has established a harmony in the body, giving special honor to that which needed it most. There was to be no want of unity in the body; all the different parts of it were to make each other's welfare their common care" (1 Cor. 12:24-25).[8] So *temperance* means to arrange and orchestrate the workings of the body's parts, enabling it to function correctly. Beds of nails and emaciating fasts are pagan, not Christian, disciplines.

Habitually Thoughtful

In *The Pilgrim's Regress*, John and Vertue listen to Mr. Sensible discourse on the good life. Mr. Sensible asserts, "Sense is easy, Reason is hard. Sense knows where to stop with gracious inconsistency, while Reason slavishly follows an abstract logic whither she knows not. The one seeks comfort and finds it, the other seeks truth and is still seeking. *Le bon sens* is the father of a flourishing family: Reason is barren and a virgin.'"[9] To add authority to his case, Mr. Sensible infers that Aristotle's "golden mean" supports his position. Vertue, however, had *read* Aristotle and noted that his "text must have differed from yours. In mine, the doctrine of the Mean does not bear the sense you have given it at all. He specially says that there is no excess of goodness. You cannot go too far in the right direction."[10]

Rather often "our Lord finds our desires not too strong, but too weak."[11] There's a *temper*, a strength, to temperance.

Reason, Lewis insisted, must rule the senses if we're to live rightly. Temperance means enjoying pleasures to the degree that they strengthen the truly good life. "Since man as such is a rational being," wrote Thomas Aquinas, "it follows that those pleasures are becoming to man which are in accordance with reason."[12]

Temperance is the only virtue that focuses only on one's self and demands "selfless self-preservation,"[13] wisely perpetuating the race and rightly enjoying pleasures of the senses. Josef Pieper summarized, "Chastity, continence, humility, gentleness, mildness, *studiositas,* are modes of realization of the discipline of temperance; unchastity, incontinence, pride, uninhibited wrath, *curiositas*, are forms of intemperance."[14] Let's use Pieper's categories to explore temperance.

Chastity

Basic to temperance is sexual self-control: chastity. Chastity describes a rightly ordered, healthy sexuality. All God created, including sexual desire, is good. So understanding our divine design, following God's law, rightly orders our sexual instinct. If a person lives "in accord with reason, he is said 'to keep himself in himself.' Unchastity destroys in a very special manner this self-possession and this human 'keeping of oneself in oneself.'"[15]

Respected historian Adolph von Harnack says the Early Church won the world to Christ through two qualities: charity and chastity. Nevertheless, C. S. Lewis said, "Chastity is the most unpopular of the Christian virtues. There is no getting away from it: the old Christian rule is 'Either marriage, with complete faithfulness to your partner, or else total abstinence.'"[16] Our world opposes Christian teachings concerning sex and, like an endless soap opera, forever misinforms us about it. Constant chatter, suggestive sex education classes, mindless magazine articles—all urge us to ignore "inhibitions" and discard scruples so we can indulge our sexual appetites.

In *Out of the Silent Planet,* Elwin Ransom noted that the planet's *hrossa* had no overpopulation problem. Asking Hyoi, a *hross,* what might happen if population out-stripped resources, Hyoi was puzzled, wondering why humans copulate more than a few times, for on Malacandra creatures conjoin only during the proper period of their lives suitable for bearing their young.

To Lewis, the Christian stance, like that of the Malacandra creatures, stresses self-control, restricting sex to marriage and acknowledging that sex is about babies, just as eating is about nourishing the body. Enjoy sexual pleasures, but always subordinate them to sex's procreative end. Remember that marriage is a sacred, God-ordained union. Marriage for Christians is holy, and adultery is evil because it severs the sexual act from the lasting personal covenant that gives it meaning.

Continence

The second aspect of temperance is continence, abstinence, restraining one's desires for pleasure. In *Perelandra,* Elwin Ransom is transported to a newly created planet, one of majestic beauty and goodness and awesome sights that "might overload the human brain."[17] Wandering in a verdant wood, he found "globes of yellow fruit" hanging from trees. Examining one, he punctured it and sipped its juice. "It was like the discovery of a totally new *genus* of pleasures, something unheard of among men, out of all reckoning, beyond all covenant. For one draught of this on earth wars would be fought and nations betrayed. It could not be classified."[18] Draining the globe, he reached for another—though he no longer needed it. But he craved the pleasure of consuming.

Soon he discovered "bubble trees," which transformed water from the ocean into fragrant perfume. He considered puncturing many of them to increase his pleasure "tenfold," but something kept him from doing so. He had all he needed, so why seek more? To restrict one's hunger for *more* suddenly seemed "a principle of far wider application and deeper moment."[19]

Ransom strolled farther, finding bushes with berries. They tasted so good, so delightful, Ransom breathed a prayer of praise for their goodness. Most of the berries, like basic bread, were not addictive. But the berries with "a bright red centre" tasted so good, he wanted to feed only on them. But the same still, small voice restrained him.

Ransom learned from the "voice" to *appropriately* enjoy the good things of Perelandra, to rightly consume what creation affords. Whether eating or drinking, sleeping or jogging, all we do should have a balance to it. The healthy life—the holy life—is a life of self-control, moderation, temperance. The purity of a holy life emerges through the *tempering* process wrought by the Holy Spirit on our spirits.

If the essence of the holy life is *loving* God with *all* one's heart, "temperance" is not a life-sucking, dour, negative spirit opposed to all pleasure. Temperance is loving our own beings, caring for our own well-being, in a righteous fashion. Unlike "self-esteem," temperance seeks self-preservation in a selfless fashion. We seek to preserve our being out of gratitude to God, who is the source of all. We seek to stay fit, like an athlete who is committed to his or her team, not out of desire for "stardom," but in order to help the team attain its goals.

Humility

"Courtly" love and poetry ever enthralled Lewis. Thus, he celebrated the "medieval ideal" of chivalry, which "taught humility and forbearance to the great warrior because everyone knew by experience how much he usually needed that lesson. It demanded valour of the urbane and modest man because everyone knew that he was as likely as not to be a milksop."[20]

The truly good man—the ideal knight—blends strength and meekness. This "is a work not of nature but of art; of that art which has human beings, instead of canvas or marble, for its medium."[21] This knightly humility characterizes temperance.

Humility has nothing to do with self-abasement or an inferiority complex. It meshes with the "high-minded man" praised by Aquinas. Such people despise small-minded evildoers. Neither fear nor flattery dislodge these people from commitment to truth and justice. Humility is revealed in one's attitude toward God, not humanity. The surrendered will denotes true humility.

Lewis noted that humility is enjoined by God because He

wants us to know Him. If we really meet Him, we'll be humbled, for all illusions of our own grandeur will fade like colored fabric in the sun. In humility, we discard the "false self" that pretends to be the center of the universe. Truly humble people never pretend to be nonentities. They're typically cheerful, fully absorbed in their work and the world around them, as blissfully unaware of their dignity as children at play.

Gentleness

After years of opposition from Oxford professors who denied him the position of professor, Lewis was offered this position at Cambridge University. He ironically noted that "it means rather less work for rather more pay." But he further explained why he looked forward to the Cambridge opportunity, for it was small, "old fashioned, and pious, and gentle and conservative—unlike this leftist, atheist, cynical, hard-boiled, huge Magdalen. Perhaps from being the fogey and 'old woman' here I shall become the *enfant terrible* there."[22]

Lewis appreciated the courtly, gentle atmosphere he believed should characterize any good society, any healthy association of people. This kind of world is portrayed by the community that assembled at St. Anne's-on-the-Hill, drawn together by Elwin Ransom in *That Hideous Strength*. Here we find the "good" people—simple, gentle souls like Mother Dimble—who prayerfully struggled against evil forces at N.I.C.E.

In the concluding Narnian chronicle, *The Last Battle,* when the "last battle" was literally beginning, Aslan's beleaguered corps, following King Tirian, suddenly faced a treacherous group of dwarfs who began shooting arrows at the talking horses, who were coming to reinforce the King's army. Angered by the betrayal, Eustace screamed, "Little swine . . . Dirty, filthy, treacherous little brutes."[23] Even the loyal unicorn, Jewel, wanted to attack the dwarfs. "But Tirian, with his face as stern as stone, said, 'Stand fast, Jewel. If you must weep, sweetheart (this was to Jill), turn your face aside and see you wet not your bowstring. And peace, Eustace. Do not scold, like a kitchen-girl. No warrior scolds. Courteous words or else hard knocks are his only language.'"[24]

"Courteous words" or "hard knocks" characterized the medieval knights Lewis celebrated. Asking whether this medieval trait is "relevant" to the modern world, Lewis answered, "It is terribly relevant." The chivalrous ideal, however imperfectly lived out in the Middle Ages, was and is a marvelous goal for humankind. "It may or may not be possible to produce by the thousand men who combine the two sides of Lancelot's character. But if it is not possible, then all talk of any lasting happiness or dignity in human society is pure moonshine."[25]

Studiositas

We must contrast the final trait of temperance, *studiositas,* with its evil counterpart, *curiositas,* which is an unhealthy desire to know what we should not know. As a part of the *philosophia perennis* Lewis advocated, *studiositas* takes the position "that rationality is at least potentially capable of giving us a true picture of reality if we commit ourselves to consistency and non-contradiction."[26] In Lewis's final space fiction, *That Hideous Strength,* Mark Studdock, held captive in a N.I.C.E. cell, is interrogated by Frost (a Freudian-type member of the "inner ring" of the utopian technocratic organization). When Mark refers to a way of determining whether or not something is "good," Frost speaks for modernity, dismissing such questions as remnants of an antiquated Aristotelian way of thinking. Folks like Frost believe the world is made up of matter-in-motion, which explains everything when fully embraced. "Good" is what works, what succeeds, in the physical world.[27]

Frost's philosophy is the "Faustian Bargain"—selling our souls to the devil to acquire magical or manipulative skills. Goethe portrayed Faust as a scholar wanting useful knowledge (*libido sciendi*) more than moral knowledge (*philo sophia).* Such moral knowledge has been largely lost. Had the classical virtues been upheld, the quest for knowledge would have been limited to *studiositas.* Unfortunately the quest has been dominated by *curiositas*—the insatiable desire to fully fathom, to tear apart, to destroy the living world. *Curiositas,* the "concupiscence of the eyes," is less interested in *what* one sees than in the self-seeking *pleasure* it affords him or her.

"I agree Technology is *per se* neutral," Lewis wrote to Arthur C. Clarke in 1943, "but a race devoted to the increase of its own power by technology with complete indifference to ethics *does* seem to me a cancer in the Universe."[28] He felt a radical change occurred in the world 200 years ago as the technological revolution, the "birth of the machines,"[29] transformed all areas of life.

When mindlessly embraced, technology becomes the "cancer" portrayed as N.I.C.E., the evil center of scientism in *That Hideous Strength*. This is evident when a demonic architect at N.I.C.E., Lord Feverstone, explained the scientific objectives of the institute—to help an elite, powerful oligarchy gain control of society. Asked what policies it would institute, Feverstone proposed sterilizing the handicapped, eliminating inferior racial groups, breeding humans like stallions and steers.

When Mark exclaimed, "This is stupendous," Feverstone agreed. At last an enlightened elite could remake the human species and control the globe.

Such "new men" would finally rule a barren planet, for another N.I.C.E. insider said the planet would be shorn—much as Delilah shaved Samson's locks—of all vegetation. Such utopian visions forever seek to undo creation to redo it to our standards. Lewis believed that much of what troubles our world derives from this desire—from our failure to grasp the nature of nature, the truth of creation.

Ransom and the community of St. Anne's cultivated *sapientia,* the learning Lewis sought to propagate in his writing. This included the temperance we need to restrain our abuse of creation. We should discipline ourselves and restrain our appetites, not to demonstrate our strength, but to have the strength to win the prize. Temperance wants to *be* good, not merely to *look* good. So Paul, writing to the Corinthians, declared,

> Do you not know that those who run in a race all run, but one receives the prize? Run in such a way that you may obtain it. And everyone who competes for the prize is temperate in all things. Now they do it to obtain a perishable crown, but we for an imperishable crown. Therefore I run thus: not with uncertainty. Thus I fight: not as one who beats the air. But I discipline my body and bring it into subjection, lest, when I have preached to others, I myself should become disqualified *(1 Cor. 9:24-27, NKJV).*

12 ✍ Faith

"The Power to Go on Believing"

*Faith in Christ is the only thing to save you . . .
and out of that Faith in Him good actions
must inevitably come.*[1]

WHEN C. S. LEWIS moved late in life from Oxford to Cambridge University, where he assumed a chair as professor of medieval and Renaissance literature, his inaugural lecture lamented the "un-christening" of Europe and defended the "old Western culture" he admired. Lewis joined a chorus of classical scholars who insisted the modern world faced a momentous crisis of faith. He recognized that the "Age of Faith"—his beloved medieval world—was largely buried and that a "post-Christian" culture triumphed in the 20th century. With the arrival of the technological society "the greatest change in the history of Western Man" had occurred.[2]

Lewis believed the Christian apprehension of reality, majestically synthesized in the Age of Faith, had ennobled humanity and society. Without the principles people had followed for more than a millennium, the world of Augustine and Aquinas and Chaucer and Shakespeare would vanish completely. What made the medieval Age of Faith admirable was its conviction that the invisible God mysteriously reveals himself to us clearly enough to elicit our saving belief in Him. Augustine formulated three critical *credere* or forms of faith:

> *Deo credere, Deum credere, in Deum credere. Deo credere* means: to believe that what God says is true . . . thus we also believe a man, whereas we do not believe "in" a man.

127

Deum credere means to believe that he is God. *In Deum credere* means: believingly to love, believingly to go to him, believingly to cling to him and be joined to his members.[3]

Deo credere: to believe what God says is true. For some, as Huck Finn quipped, faith is "believing what you know ain't so."

But Christian faith is not mindless zeal. "Blind faith" rarely guides us right. To call this "faith" maligns it. Believing everything we're told leads to fanaticism. Religious fanaticism, what Paul labeled "zeal without knowledge," often leads to disaster and death.

The virtues of faith and prudence (practical wisdom) do not conflict. Wisdom and faith walk arm in arm on the journey toward heaven. Faith, however, is a *supernatural* virtue. Such faith recognizes a "higher authority," a superior intelligence, One whose word deserves belief. So in part, real faith is *intellectual*, a mental *assent* to certain truths about reality.

Lewis insisted we define faith as an "intellectual virtue." It's faith that enables us to persevere, holding to the truth of what we've known and experienced despite times of doubt and tides of misfortune.

A delightful illustration of this forms a central thread in *The Silver Chair*. At the beginning of the story, Jill meets Aslan, who gives her a dangerous assignment: to find and rescue Prince Rilian. To accomplish her task, Aslan told her to remember four signs that would provide guidance. "Say them to yourself," he urged, "when you wake in the morning and when you lie down at night, and when you wake in the middle of the night. And whatever strange things may happen to you, let nothing turn your mind from following the Signs."[4]

Unfortunately, during their journey, Jill and her friends nearly forgot the signs. The signs didn't always seem relevant to what they were doing. But Puddleglum, the Marsh-wiggle, reminded them that they couldn't escape their obligation to follow "the Sign."[5] When they did so, even when it seemed absurd, they persevered and found Prince Rilian. Aslan's words, while not always clear, must always be heeded.

That's hearing and heeding God's instructions! And that's a basic component of true faith that saves the Narnian heroes. So we have signs, divine disclosures, which provide instructions, knitting together the soul's muscles and giving strength and flexibility to Christian faith. Our moods rise and fall like ocean tides. To sustain our faith, we must daily remind ourselves of *what* we believe. Reading, prayer, church attendance sustain the life of the spirit. Such activities routinely remind us of what we believe, the content of our faith.

Augustine wrote, "To believe is nothing other than to think with assent. Believers are also thinkers: in believing they think and in thinking they believe. If faith does not think, it is nothing."[6]

Similarly, Thomas Aquinas said, "Now the act of believing is an act of the intellect assenting to the Divine truth."[7] Drawing upon Aquinas, Lewis noted, "Revelation, he tells us in the *Summa Contra Gentiles*, is simply the communication of a spiritual inner light whereby human cognition is enabled to observe something that would otherwise remain in darkness."[8] In the language of medieval theology, it's the *fides quae creditur*—the faith that is believed, the truth that stands revealed to us, the real North Star that will guide us safely to heaven.

So faith is not a homemade fantasy. Some people think faith means imagining something they want and then claiming it's a fact—saying so makes it so! They profess a faith that can automatically cure cancer or deliver a new Mercedes, resolve all conflicts or release all tensions. This is the fraudulent faith of popular gurus who urge us to "create your own reality"—to engage in self-talk that reshapes the world.

A scene in George Orwell's *1984* illustrates this. The rebel who defies "Big Brother, Winston Smith, has been captured and tortured, strapped to a chair with electrodes strategically placed to deliver painful shocks. His inquisitor, O'Brien, says, "You believe that reality is something objective, external, existing in its own right. . . . But I tell you, Winston, that reality is not external. Reality exists in the human mind, and nowhere else." To prove his point, O'Brien holds up four fingers. "How many fingers am I holding up, Winston?" "Four," Winston replied. O'Brien then increases the voltage in the wires attached to Smith's body, sending surges of electrical current through his prisoner's frame. "How many fingers, Smith?" "Four! Four! What else can I say?" says Winston as he writhes and screams in pain. Finally O'Brien turns the dial to its highest mark, delivers the charge, and watches Winston wilt and beg for mercy.

O'Brien again holds up four fingers, asking how many. Winston replies, "I don't know. I don't know. Four, five, six—in all honesty I don't know." "Better," said O'Brien.[9]

The O'Briens of the world—Satan's corps of liars—would like us to believe that reality lies only in our minds. Sophisticated professors glibly declare, "The truth is that there is no truth." So we now find students questioning whether there is any historical truth. Some claim the Jewish Holocaust never occurred. A Williams College student says we can never know whether Hitler exterminated six million Jews—but it is "a perfectly reasonable conceptual hallucination." If it fits the world you want to imagine, believe it. If not, decide it never happened.

But to battle for the Lord means committing our minds to objective truth. It means sharing C. S. Lewis's conviction: "If Truth is objective, if we live in a world we did not create and cannot change merely by thinking, if the world is not really a dream of our own, then the most destructive belief we could possibly believe would be the denial of this primary fact. It would be like closing your eyes while driving, or blissfully ignoring the doctor's warnings."[10]

"Truth is not an attitude. Truth is not *how* we know, truth is *what* we know."[11] Joining Aristotle and Aquinas, Lewis advocated philosophical realism, taking for granted that there's a real world apart from us that we can actually know. He repeatedly critiqued varieties of fashionable subjectivism.

Swallowing something that makes you feel good doesn't make you Christian. Just as taking a placebo instead of the real prescription may give you an emotional lift, so taking some sugar-sweet aphorisms may lift your spirits. But *feeling* good about yourself (or even Jesus) does not make you a Christian!

Deum credere: to believe that He is God. Saving faith, above all else, takes God's Word as a final revelation concerning who He is. Lewis insisted that our faith has an objective focus—He who is. Saving faith *assents* to doctrinal propositions. There is, as medieval theologians carefully explained, a *fides quae creditur*—a faith that is believed. The Christian faith holds truth-rooted content. We believe what we hold to be true. Believers forever seek to focus the lenses of their souls on a reality bigger and better than their own minds. We look to—we believe in—a reality that is revealed by the Word undergirding all realities. We really want to know *who* God is.

Saving faith, Lewis wrote, makes coherent truth claims, based upon "good evidence," whether it's metaphysical or historical or experiential. Lewis felt Christians make truth claims so "believers are not cut off from unbelievers by any portentous inferiority of intelligence or any perverse refusal to think."[12]

Jesus and His disciples didn't urge people to park their minds in some apostolic parking lot. For the Christian faith—like a compass pointing ever northward—aligns our mind with the divine design. Faith provides the recipe, the map, the instructions we need for salvation. Ultimately this comes from a nourishing communion with God.

We eat because we believe food nourishes us, that we need something from outside to enter into our body, giving it life and strength. So, too, saving faith means assenting, accepting, ingesting the truth, the spiritual food God provides. We believers firmly believe many things. We believe, for example, that the historical events in the Bible actually happened. We don't believe Jesus' incarnation—"the utterly historical and concrete reality which is at the centre of all our hope, faith, and love"—is simply a finely crafted saga.[13] Nor do we believe the Crucifixion is a marvelous myth of sacrificial love. Christians maintain that Jesus was actually nailed to a cross by real Roman soldiers on a rocky hill called Golgotha.

Commenting on Evelyn Waugh's novel *Helena,* the mother of the Emperor Constantine who made a momentous pilgrimage to the Holy Land three centuries after Christ's death, George Weigel notes that it is

> driven by the simple sturdy conviction that the truth of Christianity must be tied to a certain place, a defined time, and real lives. Helena went to the Holy Land, in a word, because of a *sacramental* conviction—that in the Christian scheme of things, salvation history is not merely an idea; rather the stuff of creation is transformed by grace into the instruments of redemption, right before our eyes.[14]

Solidly anchored and constructed like the Golden Gate Bridge, the Christian faith gives us a sturdy backbone that can resist the weight of skepticism.

If we're forever unsure, we fail to find God's plan for us. When we're paralyzed by doubt, we don't taste the good life God has for us. Ancient Greek philosopher Heraclitus said, "Knowledge of divine things is lost to us by incredulity." So if we want to know God, if we want to know His love and share His life, we need a robust faith.

Corrie ten Boom wrote, "Faith is like a radar that sees through the fog—the reality of things at a distance that the human eye cannot see." I like that!

Similarly, A. W. Tozer wrote, "Faith is simply the bringing of our minds into accord with the truth. . . . Since true faith rests upon what God is, it is of utmost importance that, to the limit of our comprehension, we know what He is. 'They that know thy name will put their trust in thee.'"[15]

Princeton University professor of philosophy Diogenes Allen responded to a person who asked, "Why should I go to church?" by saying, "Because Christianity's true."[16]

C. S. Lewis noted, "In lecturing to popular audiences I have repeatedly found it almost impossible to make them understand that I recommend Christianity because I thought its affirmations to be objectively *true.*"[17]

Such faith, Allen argues, is a "reasonable faith." Certainly there's a subjective pole to our knowing, but that doesn't eliminate the possibility of knowing *truth* embedded in our world. Reason and revelation complement each other when we experience *"metanoia,* a turning from the sensible world toward the supersensible realities on which it depends for its order and goodness."[18]

Non-Christians can obviously question the assent Christians give to doctrinal propositions. However, Lewis reasoned, they need to

> see how the assent, of necessity, moves us from the logic of speculative thought into what might perhaps be called the logic of personal relations. What would, up till then, have been variations simply of opinion become variations of conduct by a person to a Person. *Credere Deum esse* turns into *credere in Deum.* And *Deum* here is this God, the increasingly knowable Lord.[19]

So faith has another side. Beyond the head, the heart needs to embrace the truth.

In Deum credere: to believe in God. Faith possesses an active aspect. Lewis often defined faith (to use the medieval definitions) not simply as the "faith that is believed" *(fides quae creditur)* but as the *fides qua creditur*—the "faith by which (it) is believed," the faith that acts, the faith that is an act of trust. To simply *think* some things are true is not enough. Faith, as a supernatural virtue, means trust, holding on to what we believe, doing the kinds of things such belief entails. Faith includes action. That kind of faith becomes visible as we trust God. For faith is "the power of continuing to believe what we once honestly thought to be true until cogent reasons for honestly changing our minds are brought before us."[20]

We Christians admire the great men and women of our faith, the heroes of our tradition, who lived bravely and well. They *acted* out their faith. That's clear in Heb. 11. After lauding the faith in verses 1-2, the writer describes the faith that believes *(fides qua creditur)* in a long catalogue of patriarchs and saints. Faith, not feeling, enables us to persevere. Faith, not feeling, glistens like a diamond, marking the lasting commitment that typifies authentic discipleship. Faith is a quality of character, a virtuous way of living, Lewis clarified when he reminds us that we must often simply trust others who know more than we do. "In getting a dog out of a trap, in extracting a thorn from a child's finger, in teaching a boy to swim or rescuing one who can't, in getting a frightened beginner over a nasty place on a mountain, the one fatal obstacle may be their distrust."[21]

If they will not endure some pain, or uncertainty, they cannot be helped. "Sometimes," he notes, "because of their unbelief, we can do no mighty works. But if we succeed, we do so because they have maintained their faith in us against apparently contrary evidence."[22]

Finally, this "faith" trusts God to save us, understanding we fail to save ourselves. Throughout *The Chronicles of Narnia,* though the children and various animals are expected to do their best and battle for righteousness, ultimately only Aslan can save them. By *trusting* Him, even when He seems strangely absent, we find victory.

This faith is most evident in our willingness to trust God to do what He promised to do. For years I thought there was a place called New Zealand, but when I got on a plane destined for Auckland, paying money for the tickets and trusting the pilot to guide the plane, I illustrated actual faith. Try and sell me a ticket to the fabled continent of Atlantis, however, and I'll take a rain check! Thus, as Martin Luther said, "To believe in God is to go down on your knees."

No wonder Søren Kierkegaard lifted Abraham as the great "knight of faith," the hero we Christians should emulate. Oswald Chambers wrote, "If we are going to live as disciples of Jesus, we have to remember that all noble things are difficult. The Christian life is gloriously difficult, but the difficulty of it does not make us faint and cave in, it rouses us up to overcome. Do we so appreciate the marvelous salvation of Jesus that we are doing our utmost for His highest?"[23]

I'm confident many of the folks sprawled in their easy chairs watching television hour after hour do assent to the truth that exercise is good for us. They believe! They may even think they will soon get up and exercise—though they move only from chair to bed. Millions of people buy books detailing healthful diets. They think they will actually diet. But thinking about it never results in lost weight. Many troubled people seek counselors and agree with what they're told, but agreeing fails to solve their problems. No one resolves more fervently to stop drinking than a well-soused alcoholic! Alcoholics easily admit booze is bad—but such beliefs never save them from the addiction.

Simply hearing God's Word, James says, is like looking in a mirror and forgetting what we see. Real faith, saving faith, actively responds to the "Word of Truth" and *does* the Word.

13 ✍ Hope

"Something That Cannot Be Had in This World"

*At present we are on the outside of the world, the wrong side of the door. We discern the freshness and purity of morning, but they do not make us fresh and pure. We cannot mingle with the splendours we were. But all the leaves of the New Testament are rustling with the rumor that it will not always be so. Some day, God willing, we shall get **in**. When human souls have become as perfect in voluntary obedience, then they will put on its glory, or rather that greater glory of which Nature is only the first sketch.[1]*

*T*HE LATE GREAT HUMORIST *E*RMA *B*OMBECK posed a poignant question in the title of one of her books: *If Life Is a Bowl of Cherries—What Am I Doing in the Pits?* Her lighthearted query haunts the darkened cul-de-sacs of our world, where too many of us fall into the pits! And the deepest pit of all is the pit of despair, the loss of a supernatural virtue: hope.

In his early years, C. S. Lewis struggled with "a deeply ingrained pessimism; a pessimism, by that time, much more of intellect than of temper."[2] This suitably prepared him to join the "lost generation" of writers such as Ernest Hemingway and T. S. Eliot, who lamented the ills of their times. They seemed ready to paste, as a soaring banner over the century, Dante's inscription over hell's gateway: "Abandon Hope, All Ye Who Enter Here."

Once he became a Christian and was "surprised by joy," Lewis discarded his pessimism. Most of his works celebrate a robust faith and delight in the goodness of life. But at the end of his life, he struggled with unexpected hopelessness. Having married Joy Davidman, he had discovered a joy deeper than he had ever known. Then she died after a long bout with cancer. Dealing with her death, he wrote *A Grief Observed,* recording his turmoil and airing questions he debated. He wondered in the darkness, "Where is God?"[3] Even more troubling, he was tempted to "believe such dreadful things about Him."[4] He wondered if, in fact, his beloved wife still lived in heaven. Death, close at hand, proved painfully real and apparently final.

Amazingly, one of the most famous "defenders" of the Christian faith couldn't defend it while paralyzed with grief. His faith collapsed like an imploded skyscraper. "You never know how much you really believe anything," he admitted, "until its truth or falsehood becomes a matter of life and death to you."[5]

Despairing, he doubted God's goodness, wondering if all he had embraced was an illusion. Hope vanished, if only for a season. Yet however desperate the times, we hunger for a hope only God can give. And in time, Lewis recovered such hope. Perhaps "God hurts only to heal."[6] The Divine Surgeon wills to do His sanctifying work, even when it hurts us, to prepare us for His eternal world. Lewis's shallow images of joy and God needed to be shattered, for his deepest longings would be satisfied only with their reality. So as Lewis displayed, hope refined in the darkest of times sustains us by sharpening our focus on what's eternal.

Defining the Virtue

True hope, wrote Thomas Aquinas, "attains God by leaning on His help in order to obtain the hoped for good."[7] Since the ultimate good for us is God, only He can provide hope. "Such good," Aquinas continued, "is eternal life, which consists in the enjoyment of God Himself. For we should hope from Him for nothing less than Himself, since His goodness, by which He imparts good things to His creature, is no less than His essence. Therefore the proper and principle object of hope is eternal happiness."[8]

Hopelessness is darker than discouragement, for in perverse

ways, it is the worst of spiritual ills. Augustine declared, "There are two things that kill the soul, despair and false hope."[9] Both of these killers, the bottomless pits of the soul, are hopeless dark holes. Despair and presumption are the great soul killers. They're twin offspring of the most damning of all sins—giving up on God.

Despair

Some folks are so down-to-earth, so "sensible," they cannot entertain thoughts of heaven. Relying only on sense experience, refusing to believe in what they cannot see or touch, they easily despair. Turning away from Christ's redemption, the sense-shackled soul literally casts away the rope that binds him or her to God. When disillusionment is a persistent stance—not a passing mood generated by physical or emotional currents—it is especially deadly. It is, however, as Lewis noted, the most honest way to live if a person doesn't believe in eternal life.

Persistent, sustained rejection of God's forgiveness and grace, deliberately turning our back to Him and slamming the door on His love, is the truly unforgivable sin, the sin against the Holy Spirit. Damning despair won't accept the opportunity God gives us to become His children. Thus, Thomas Aquinas said it's the most "hateful" sin, since by it a person "'loses his constancy both in the every day toils of this life, and, what is worse, in the battle of faith.' And Isidore says . . . 'To commit a crime is to kill the soul, but to despair is to fall into hell.'"[10] Despair is a result of sloth, when one refuses to be holy or to accept responsibility to live magnanimously and well.

Presumption

When not despairing, people who ignore their created status slip easily into presumption. Thinking only of God's justice may plunge us into despair, but thinking only of His mercy may beget presumption. Such presumption—what Augustine called "false hope"—assumes only good can come. Both attitudes refuse to accept our *status viatoris*, our status as travelers, and both turn out to be "unnatural and deadly."[11] In Thomas Aquinas's words, immoderate hope assumes we need not "the power and mercy of God," so "if a man hopes to obtain pardon without repenting, or glory without merits. This presumption is, properly, a species of sin against the Holy Ghost, because, namely, by presuming thus a man removes or despises the assistance of the Holy Spirit, by which it is withdrawn from sin."[12] Presumption *assumes* all will be well simply because a person wants it to be. It's an overconfidence about the future. It often masquerades as hope, but in fact it's a *falsa similitudo,* a false likeness, a phony face. Fundamentally, Augustine said, presumption is a *perversa securitas,* a perverse security with no basis in fact.

One form of such presumption appeared in Pelagianism, the notion that on our own we can attain eternal life. A British monk, Pelagius, denied the doctrine of original sin, asserting that each of us is born, like Adam and Eve, without any bent to evil. We can, he said, through righteous living, through following the example of Christ, *earn* our salvation. We just need to resolve to live right and please God by doing so. So we're tempted to replace the gospel of grace with human righteousness.

Though quite "religious," Pelagians of all stripes exude pride, which Lewis often emphasized is the most deadly of all sins. Pelagianism appears, for example, when people think abstaining from liquor and tobacco—or meat and milk—makes them righteous. Pelagian presumption appears when folks think incessant church work makes them godly. Presumption shines brightly when people imagine their political correctness suffices for goodness. So many in our society think they need nothing more than sincerity and a few "random acts of kindness" to get to heaven.

The second form of presumption leans to the other extreme. Rather than eliminating grace, it eliminates human responsibility. Aquinas insisted, "To sin with the intention of persevering in sin and through the hope of being pardoned, is presumptuous, and this does not diminish, but increases sin."[13] Ignoring this truth, some intellectuals, working out implications of the Protestant Reformation, have so celebrated grace to the point that they eliminate works of love. If we are guaranteed salvation by grace through faith *alone*—if we are saved *in* our sins, simultaneously justified and sinful—it's easy to presume upon God's mercy and casually explain away sinful behavior.

Still another form of presumption, widely shared in our day, is universalism, the comforting view that somehow everyone will ultimately be saved. Since God is love, universalists insist, He could never actually allow anyone to suffer hell's punishment. To those who object to God's promise to punish sinners, C. S. Lewis wisely wrote, "'What are you asking God to do?' To wipe out their past sins, and, at all costs, to give them a fresh start, smoothing every difficulty and offering every miraculous help? But He has done so, on Calvary. To forgive them? They will not be forgiven. To leave them alone? Alas, I am afraid that is what He does."[14]

In another place, Lewis wrote, "It's not a question of God 'sending' us to Hell. In each of us there is something growing up which will of itself *be Hell* unless it is nipped in the bud. The matter is serious: let us put ourselves in His hands at once—this very day, this hour."[15]

For us, "there is often an escape from this Hell, but there is never more than one—the way of humiliation, repentance, and (where possible) restitution."[16]

Resurrection Anticipation

Unlike either despair or presumption, Christian hope focuses on an anticipated life everlasting through the resurrection of Jesus Christ. With Aristotle, Lewis believed that nature makes nothing in vain. Hungers point to real things that satisfy them. Babies want mother's milk, and it's there. Rabbits want to mate, and they do so, making more rabbits. We desire love, and when we find it, we know it's real. So if we have longings for a better world, longings for eternal life, it's likely we're designed "for another world."[17]

We're made for better things! So, we need to keep the fire of hope burning, moving toward that eternal realm Jesus prepared for us. In his majestic meditation on death and immortality, Paul declared, "If in this life only we have hope in Christ, we are of all men most miserable. But now is Christ risen from the dead, and become the firstfruits of them that slept" (1 Cor. 15:19-20, KJV). Accordingly, the virtue of hope is no more escapist than a young woman's hope for a wedding. It's perfectly normal because it flows out of who we are and what we're meant to be. We can keep busy, working to make this world good—as do many unmarried women—without deleting our desire for something even better. In the Christian tradition, heavenly-minded saints have quite often radically reformed their world.

Worldliness Threatens

Interestingly enough, Satan seeks to dispel hope by getting us overly attached to earthly things. The demonic Screwtape said God continually reminded earthlings of their eternal destiny. Young folks, like colts frisking in a pasture, easily abandon themselves to adventures, romance, music, and poetry. Longevity, long tenure in the world, however, often dulls their sensitivities. Time washes away the hunger for *heaven!*

In truth, Christians should grow more hopeful as they get older. This is because they understand, with Augustine, that "God is younger than all else."[18] Thus we find, as we study the saints of the past, their surprising youthfulness in old age. There is—or should be—a divine youthfulness that results from sharing the "life of God, who is closer and more intimate to us than we are to ourselves."[19] Longing for everlasting life, saints exude a youthfulness that, like daily polished silver, softly shimmers. Like Mother Teresa, they launch building programs and establish hospitals for the sick or orphanages for abandoned children. Saints waste no time reliving past triumphs or regretting ancient tragedies, for they always have work to do in Christ's kingdom.

Such holiness disdains worldliness. But it's not a trivialized worldliness reduced to dress and diet. The worldliness that wars with holiness is the attitude that fastens, as if with a long lag bolt, our attention singularly on this world and its dividends. "Worldly" people refuse to accept their *status viatoris,* the condition of "being on the way." Worldly people want to enjoy "the good life" here and now. Their hopes focus on higher salaries, larger homes, nicer cars. Worldly people turn away from their true nature, their designed destiny. They refuse to humbly accept God's design for humanity; they dull the deepest desire of the human heart: heaven. Since all that is "fully real is Heavenly," Lewis insisted earthly things, physical pleasures cannot fully satisfy us. What they do is awaken us to those permanent things that ultimately will. They're a bit like icons, windows to our heavenly home.

Consequently, we who hope live not for time but for eternity. Turning from sin and death and all that *is not,* we faithfully march toward what eternally *is,* what is forever *good,* God. Vital Christian hope finds joy in living for a future ordained by God. This is the virtue that sustains pilgrims as they struggle through the sloughs of despair or engage in the "last battle" against hell's forces. Hope sustains believers, for it is a supernatural gift, an infused virtue, by which they look forward to eternal life. It's all of grace!

Vanquishing Death

Above all, hope enables us to face, honestly and well, the reality of death. Facing death, Lewis wrote, we recognize that "nothing, not even the best and noblest, can go on as it now is. Nothing, not even what is lowest and most bestial, will not be raised again if it submits to death. It is sown a natural body, it is raised a spiritual body. Flesh and blood cannot come to the Mountains [heaven]. Not because they are too rank, but because they are too weak."[20]

Death surrounds us. The cosmos cools; nothing lasts forever. We naturally look elsewhere for better things. The longing for other worlds, the *Sehnsucht* that so early entranced Lewis, found focus in his Christian writings, in a longing for heaven.

Time magazine devoted its September 8, 1947, cover story to C. S. Lewis. The article indicated that Lewis considered heaven "a state as real as Sunday morning breakfast."[21] Indeed, he wrote, "I suspect that our conception of Heaven as *merely* a state of mind is not unconnected with the fact that the specifically Christian virtue of Hope has in our own time grown so languid."[22] This conviction is amplified in *The Great Divorce,* in which Lewis speaks through the character of George Macdonald, declaring, "Heaven is reality itself. All that is fully real is Heavenly. For all that can be shaken will be shaken and only the unshakable remains."[23]

Lest we think the desire to satisfy natural desires resembles taking a bribe, we must remember "either there is 'pie in the sky' or there is not. If there is not, then Christianity is false, for this doctrine is woven into its whole fabric."[24]

Heaven is designed for spiritually-minded believers, so "it is safe to tell the pure in heart that they shall see God, for only the pure in heart want to."[25] For himself, Lewis said, "There have been times when I think we do not desire heaven but more often I find myself wondering whether, in our heart of hearts, we have ever desired anything else."[26]

This truth pervades *The Chronicles of Narnia,* in which Aslan's subjects often long for "Aslan's Land" or "Aslan's Mountain." To be with Aslan is, fundamentally, what makes everything we do ultimately worthwhile. Yet "Aslan's Land" is also a beautiful world of towering mountains, gentle breezes, dancing waterfalls, of rich forests and flowered meadows. The mouse Reepicheep, in *The Voyage of "The Dawn Treader,"* hopes to reach that marvelous world—and departs to it at the story's end. As the moment approaches, the crew felt they'd entered a new, uncharted realm. They needed less sleep; the sun was larger; the water was clearer; great white birds sang songs everyone understood.

Then Reepicheep jumped overboard, much to everyone's consternation. Back on board, he declared the water was "sweet." This confirmed an ancient prophecy he recited. When King Caspian drank the water, he noted, "It—it's like light more than anything else."[27] And Reepicheep concurred: "Drinkable light. We must be very near the end of the world now."[28] As others drank, they relished its loveliness, its goodness. All things seemed transformed into potable light.

For many days the *Dawn Treader* sailed eastward. The light grew more luminous, lighter than light! In time the water became so shallow the ship could go no farther. Then Sir Reepicheep got into a small boat with a few of the crew and ventured toward the world's end.

Then the water grew too shallow for even the small boat. "'This,' said Reepicheep, 'is where I go on alone.'"[29] He got into his tiny coracle and soon vanished from sight, entering Aslan's land.

The final Narnian chronicle, *The Last Battle,* one of Lewis's masterpieces, gives us the clearest picture of Aslan's Land, the hoped-for ultimate end for all of us. After the battle, just when Aslan's small company had apparently lost all, a magical opening appeared—a doorway leading from a stable to another world. As the redeemed creatures moved through it, they were awed at the land's grandeur. As they moved "further up and further in," they noted how aspects of the new land resembled old Narnia. The Unicorn said, "I have come home at last! This is my real country! I belong here. This is the land I have been looking for all my life, though I never knew it till now. The reason why we loved the old Narnia is that it sometimes looked a little like this."[30]

As they finally finish their journey, they are reunited with friends from earlier days. Leading those welcoming them, as you might guess, is Sir Reepicheep, courtly as ever, assuring them that they're home.

As fairy tales teach us, we need to break the evil spell of worldliness that encrusts earthlings. Lewis lamented the "worldliness that has been laid upon us for nearly a hundred years. Almost our whole education has been directed to silencing this shy, persistent, inner voice; almost all our modern philosophies have been devised to convince us that nothing but earthly realities exist."[31]

But actually, to Lewis, the pleasures we experience in this life, the goods that truly appease us for a moment, are dull foretastes of what will come, for we will drink from the very Source of all good that pleases. And "that, I believe, is what lies before us. The whole man is to drink joy from the fountain of joy."[32] That's our hope! "For we are saved by hope: but hope that is seen is not hope: for what a man seeth, why doth he yet hope for? But if we hope for that we see not, then do we with patience wait for it" (Rom. 8:24-25, KJV).

14 ✐ Love

"An Affair of the Will"

*If you continue to love Jesus, nothing much
can go wrong with you, and I hope
you may always do so.*[1]

*T*HE THIRD OF THE SUPERNATURAL VIRTUES—like a Concorde jetliner soaring through the stratosphere—is love, the divinely infused habit by which a person loves God and his or her neighbor. It's the capstone of the virtuous life for Christians, the central chord of the holiness ethic. And love is certainly central to the ethics of C. S. Lewis, for "every Christian would agree that a man's spiritual health is exactly proportional to his love for God."[2]

Toward the end of *The Pilgrim's Regress,* the young pilgrim, John, and his companion, Vertue, had learned to "see nothing now but realities." Then their guide explained that one of the apparent "wise" men they encountered, "Mr. Sensible," aired superficial learning. Though he cited impressive classical sources, he had only sampled them without absorbing their truth. "He did not learn them. He learned only catchwords from them."[3] He referred to Rabelais's motto, "Do what you will," but didn't note that Rabelais was quoting Augustine's phrase, "Love and do as you will," which duplicated Jesus' words: "On these two commandments hang all the law and the prophets" (Matt. 22:40, KJV). Love, and do as you will. Yes, without question! But not just any love suffices. Only *agape* love, divine love, the love that is holy as God is holy, fully enables us to live right.

144

Its Origin: The God Who Is Love

The love that infuses true virtue comes from above. "The love of God is shed abroad in our hearts by the Holy Ghost" (Rom. 5:5, KJV). Lewis noted that "William Morris wrote a poem called 'Love Is enough' and someone is said to have reviewed it briefly in the words 'It isn't.'"[4]

Christians believe the biblical proposition that "God is love" (1 John 4:8), not the popular nostrum that "Love is God."

Too many of us thoughtlessly reduce God to the personification of an admirable human trait—love. But, to Lewis, when we say "God is love," we proclaim something utterly unique to Christianity, for if God is love, He is a Person who initiates relationships and interacts with others, establishing covenants with His people. It's part of a dance of love featuring the Holy Spirit, pure Love, who throughout all eternity works with the Father and the Son.

So all we need—love included—comes from God. Our "human loves can be glorious images of Divine love. No less than that: but also no more."[5] His love, *agape*—not an emotion we pump up regarding Him or others—provides the source for all that makes love good. Importantly, as George Macdonald wrote, God's love "is a consuming fire" that is "so terribly pure that it destroys all that is not pure as fire, which demands like purity in our worship. He will have purity."[6]

Love's Seat: Our Will

The love of God, the love that has divine roots, indwells our will. As Lewis understood, Christian love—or charity—is not emotional, not an elusive feeling, but volitional, the resolve of the will. We decide to serve God or help our brothers—to tithe our income or serve as a missionary. It's the decision, the act, not the emotion, that is love.

To be a whole person, to be what the ancient Romans called *homo humanus*—a person of integrity or a holy person—means to shift our attention from private pleasures and sheltered treasures to what's good for others. We want them to live right instead of cleverly. We love them, not when we want what may please or profit them, but when we seek what's morally and spiritually good for them. Love's not an emotional response to what pleases us, but a deliberate commitment to the well-being of others.

This act of the will is more than the empathetic compassion or easy-going kindness that sometimes passes for love. To will another's *good* may not always appear kind to him or her. Sentimental kindness wants others to be "happy; not happy in this way or in that, but just happy."[7] Love, however, wills our neighbor's *good,* so it may at times impose penalties, prescribe painful medicines, and make the beloved unhappy! So Josef Pieper says, love is not

> undifferentiated approval of everything the beloved person thinks and does in real life. As a corollary, love is also not synonymous with the wish for the beloved to feel good always and in every situation and for him to be spared experiencing pain or grief in all circumstances. "Mere 'kindness' which tolerates anything except [the beloved's] suffering" has nothing to do with real love.[8]

Augustine insisted that we must never think love is "abject and sluggish," a passive "gentleness" that refuses to discipline children or rebuke neighbors. Such is not "charity, but mere feebleness." Love persons, but not their evil behavior. "Love that which God made, love not that which the man himself made."[9]

So love neither tolerates evil nor excuses sin. Lovers want what's truly *good* for their beloved—not what feels good. We find in *The Great Divorce* a portrait, described earlier in this book, of motherly love that isn't love at all. Pam, one of the "ghosts," wants to see her son, Michael, whose death she had long lamented. She had indulged in a "ten years' ritual of grief. Keeping his room exactly as he'd left it: keeping anniversaries: refusing to leave the house" so as to indulge her sorrow.[10] She proclaimed her love for her son, but heaven's spokesman (George Macdonald) informed her that God wanted her to love him as God willed, not as she desired. She responded as defensively as a chastened adolescent, insisting that as a mother, her love was the finest feeling imaginable. But Macdonald declared, feelings, as feelings, may be either good or bad, saintly or sinful. Only "when God's hand is on the rein," do they become holy. They turn evil when they metamorphose "into false gods."[11]

Self-righteously relishing her misconstrued love, the mournful

Pam insisted she was right and noble. Anger overcame her as she demanded God return her son. Arrogant to the end, Pam refused to leave her hell of self-pity. Her "God of Love," like sentimental mantras celebrating a "gentle Jesus, meek and mild," was simply her own fabrication of a God who soothes all sorrows without demanding any transformation of character. Explaining heaven's decree, Macdonald said that "love, as mortals understand the word, isn't enough."[12] Only as it's planted, buried like seed corn, can it come alive and send forth shoots of righteousness.

True love—the love that is an act of the will—is an act of obedience, ever aware of God's ultimate Goodness. When we believe this, when *by our lives* we validate this belief, we reaffirm and reestablish the covenant relationship with God that is one of Scripture's grand themes. Unlike legal contracts, with their payments and penalties, covenants establish personal bonds between consenting people. Covenants contain personal commitments, freely upheld in loving ways. A covenant, like a marriage vow, entails *serving,* joining with, lovingly *submitting* to another. It's evident in what Lewis calls "Gift-love" rather than "Need-love." As he explained, Need-love wants things from God, but Gift-love volunteers for service. Need-love laments, but Gift-love praises. Need-love wants the Lover ever at hand, but Gift-love rejoices to know He simply *is.*

What we find, when we really love, is that it often costs us more than we imagined. We want its sweet consolations, and they are certainly abundant. But we also discover its pain. To fall in love is delightful. To hold your wife's hand as she's dying, after 50 years of marriage, hurts more intensely than heart surgery. To begin pastoring a congregation generally brings sweet satisfaction in the early days. But after a decade, a loving pastor will wear the scars of criticism as well as the crowns of praise. The very goodness of love guarantees its depths as well as heights. So, Lewis warned, if we love, we will suffer. We can "wrap it carefully round with hobbies and little luxuries; avoid all entanglements; lock it up safe in the casket or coffin of your selfishness. But in that casket—safe, dark, motionless, airless—it will change. It will not be broken; it will become unbreakable, impenetrable, irredeemable. The alternative to tragedy, or at least to the risk of tragedy, is damnation. The only place outside

Heaven where you can be perfectly safe from all the dangers and perturbations of love is Hell."[13]

Love Delights in Its Beloved's Being

A great consensus has developed in the writings of our wisest interpreters of love. Thomas Aquinas tells us, "The first thing that a lover 'wills' is for the beloved to exist and live. The 'I' who loves above all wants the existence of the 'You.'"[14] Real love wraps supportive arms around the beloved, seeking to sustain his or her existence, committed to enriching and unleashing his or her freely developing being. Similarly, Lewis says, our love of beauty has a certain "disinterested" quality.

A good person would neither deface the Mona Lisa nor bulldoze Mont Blanc. Unseen wilderness areas, verdant gardens in distant lands, delight him. One who is *good* rejoices to declare things of truth and beauty "very good."[15]

In the beginning, the God who is love said, "Let there be." The Wisdom of Solomon says, "God created all things that they might be" (Wisd. of Sol. 1:14). Thus, an ancient precept declared, *omne ens est bonum*—"all being is good." God loved so much that He gave *being* to all that *is*. Consequently, when we love as God loves, we want to recognize and revere the *being* of what we love. "What matters to us, beyond mere existence, is the explicit confirmation 'It is *good* that you exist; how wonderful that you are!'"[16] It's what a newly engaged person feels about his or her fiancé: how wonderful you are, and how wonderful it is that you are!

Loving God's Creatures

If we love something simply because it *is,* if we love God just because He *is,* we love them for their *being.* It's like standing back, awed by the majesty of Chartres's cathedral or the glory of Mont Blanc, and rejoicing simply to be in their presence. Love seeks not to remodel the beloved in accord with some elusive ideal, or to reduce it to a carbon copy of one's own portrait. Love delights to let things be. Laying aside the concave mirrors of self-scrutiny, loving eyes look outward and see others most clearly. Love appreciates the uniqueness, the complexity, the abiding mystery of its beloved. Love wills another's well-being by preserving and delighting in it. Lewis said:

I think God wants us to love Him more, not to love creatures (even animals) less. We love everything in one way too much (i.e. at the expense of our love for Him) but in another way we love everything too little.[17]

This means we need to cultivate what Augustine called "ordinate loves," rightly loving all things. Lewis believed that love for animals, love for mountains, love for anything *other than* ourselves, takes us toward God. If creation is God's handiwork, taking delight in it clarifies certain truths about Him. Saintly Christians have frequently found clear parallels between the book of Scripture and the book of nature. As Augustine said, "All creatures contain the traces of the trinity."[18] A fine biography of Lewis, *Jack,* portrays him as delighting in the holiness of creation. "Jack perceived the divine in both the scenery and in this ruined building [Tintern Abbey] that had been blessed by time: 'Anything like the *sweetness* and peace of the long shafts of sunlight falling through the window on this grass cannot be imagined. All churches should be roofless. A holier place I never saw.'"[19] His "view of nature was essentially mystical. He often saw it in 'the signature of all things.'"[20] Thus, in one of his later works, Lewis declared:

It is well to have specifically holy places, and things, and days, for, without these focal points or reminders, the belief that all is holy and "big with God" will soon dwindle into a mere sentiment. But if these holy places, things, and days cease to remind us, if they obliterate our awareness that all ground is holy and every bush (could we but perceive it) a Burning Bush, then the hallows begin to do harm. Hence both the necessity, and the perennial danger, of "religion."[21]

In *The Four Loves,* however, Lewis cautions against confusing love for nature with higher forms of love. Nature lovers like William Wordsworth exalted in a certain mood, which may be fine so long as it is not elevated into divinity. Nature itself, Lewis believed, certainly illustrates important truths. But it is not the truth.

One may certainly validate in nature what he or she knows through philosophy or revelation. And wise souls often nourish their understanding through the contemplation of creation.

Lewis sought to love God and all His creatures, great and small. And he urges us to make love our daily routine, for "good and evil both increase at compound interest. That is why the little decisions you and I make every day are of such infinite importance."[22]

The cup of water, the passing smile, the hardly noticed gestures of love shed abroad the reality of holiness. We're to love *particular* beings, not abstractions. We encounter in *Out of the Silent Planet* and *Perelandra* the evil physicist Weston, who fanatically loves humanity. Yet he's ready to kill individuals and innocent creatures to secure the survival of his own species. Weston, like many utopians, feels love for humanity in the abstract but has little sympathy or concern for specific, living individuals.

Though less spectacularly than Moses at the burning bush on Mount Sinai, when we love, we see things aglow with the light of God's presence, marked by the Creator's touch. It is what ecstatic parents sometimes feel when they first see their newborn child—according to one survey the "happiest day" in a mom's or dad's life. On a spiritual plane, following their "new birth," many Christians have recorded how nature seemed transformed and "new" as well—stars shined brighter, trees glimmered greener, birds sang sweeter than ever before. The divine power that inwardly transformed them radiated equally in their surroundings.

Varied Manifestations: Four Loves

Lewis's *The Four Loves* provides readers with an exemplary discussion of this subject. Lewis takes the Greek language's terms for "love" and grants us insight into its variegated splendor. First he distinguishes between "Gift love," "Need love," and "Appreciative love," insisting that each is proper in its own realm. Then he turns to the first of the four loves, *storge,* affection, "the humblest and most widely diffused of loves."[23]

This is the love parents instinctively feel for their children, the love that binds together brothers and sisters who live in the same home. It's an at-home, common love that has no desire to harm. Good *storge* seeks "its own abdication," just as parents and teachers seek to ultimately make themselves superfluous.[24] Children need to grow up and live on their own; students need to master materials and move on beyond their teachers.

Storge—affection—loves by helping the beloved attain his or her true end as a person.

The second form of love, *philia*, friendship, was prized by the ancients, such as Aristotle, who devoted two books of his *Nichomachean Ethics* to the subject. It has often been neglected by moderns. Whereas *storge* is the most natural, almost inescapable, of loves, *philia* is the least natural, the most freely chosen. Friends become friends because they share common interests, ranging from golf to poetry to antique cars. A circle of friends, like a rubber band, is warmly elastic, expanding to admit almost any number of friends who choose to join the endeavor. It's the least possessive of loves, the least needy of them all.

As Lewis discusses friendship, we can almost feel the presence of his fellow "Inklings" (J. R. R. Tolkien, Charles Williams, and others) who gathered together weekly to discuss their writing and to simply enjoy companionship.

Whereas *philia* is the least possessive of loves, *eros*, the love between a man and woman, is the most possessive, the most intensely focused. *Eros* must never be confused with *venus*; love is not lust. Unfortunately, in our society, magazines and movies, novels and sitcoms, tempt us to equate *eros* with sex. There is, however, a vast difference. For "sexual desire, without Eros, wants *it*, the *thing in itself*; Eros wants the Beloved."[25]

Lovers in love want to possess, to live with, to live for, another person—a specific person. Lovers want a person, not pleasure with a person. Consequently, *eros* ever makes promises. "Love makes vows unasked; can't be deterred from making them. 'I will be ever true,' are almost the first words he utters. Not hypocritically but sincerely."[26] *Eros* freely offers to enter a lasting covenant, a commitment designed to last forever.

Fourth, there's *agape*, charity. Of all the loves, it's the most clearly supernatural. This is infused by God's Spirit, something we receive by grace alone. Just as God became Man in Christ Jesus, assuming unto himself human nature, so charity assumes the natural loves, elevating and integrating them into aspects of *agape*.[27] Only it endures. It's the greatest of all, the end of all loves.

Indeed, as Paul insisted, "the most excellent way" (1 Cor. 12:31), is the *agape* way. For "now abideth faith, hope, charity, these three; but the greatest of these is charity" (1 Cor. 13:13, KJV).

Notes

Preface

1. Alastair MacIntyre, *After Virtue: A Study in Moral Theory,* 2nd ed. (Notre Dame, Ind.: University of Notre Dame Press, 1984), 263.

2. Ibid.

3. David Wells, *Losing Our Virtue* (Grand Rapids: William B. Eerdmans Publishing Co., 1998), 1.

4. Robert Bork, "Hard Truth About America," *The Christian Activist* 7 (October 1995): 1, quoted in ibid., 453.

5. Wells, *Losing Our Virtue,* 13.

6. Ibid., 3.

7. Ibid., 180.

8. Ibid., 206.

9. James Davison Hunter, *The Death of Character: Moral Education in an Age Without Good and Evil* (New York: Basic Books, 2000), 13.

10. Ibid., xiii.

11. Ibid., xv.

12. Ibid., 9.

13. Ibid., xv.

14. John Stackhouse Jr., "Movers and Shapers of Modern Evangelicals," *Christianity Today,* September 16, 1996, 59.

15. Chuck Colson, "The Oxford Prophet," *Christianity Today,* June 15, 1998, 72.

16. Ibid.

17. Ibid.

Introduction

1. C. S. Lewis, "Myth Became Fact," in *God in the Dock: Essays on Theology and Ethics* (Grand Rapids: William B. Eerdmans Publishing Co., 1970), 66.

2. C. S. Lewis, "The Inner Ring," in *The Weight of Glory* (New York: Macmillan Co., 1965), 93.

3. Quoted in James Como, *Branches to Heaven: The Geniuses of C. S. Lewis* (Dallas: Spence Publishing Co., 1998), 59. *Opus dei* means "work of God."

4. Walter Hooper, introduction to *Weight of Glory,* xv.

5. Neville Coghill, "The Approach to English," in *Light on C. S. Lewis,* ed. Jocelyn Gibb (London: Geoffrey Bles, 1965), 64.

6. Michael Aeschliman, *The Restitution of Man* (Grand Rapids: William B. Eerdmans Publishing Co., 1983), 3-4.

7. C. S. Lewis, "The Poison of Subjectivism," in *Christian Reflections* (Grand Rapids: William B. Eerdmans Publishing Co., 1967), 73.

8. Ibid.

9. C. S. Lewis, *The Pilgrim's Regress: An Allegorical Apology for Christianity, Reason, and Romanticism* (London: Geoffrey Bles Ltd., 1933; reprint, Grand Rapids: William B. Eerdmans Publishing Co., 1965), 130.

10. Gerhard Niemeyer, *Within and Above Ourselves* (Wilmington, Del.: ISI Books, 1997), 281.

11. Lewis, *That Hideous Strength* (1946; reprint, New York: Macmillan Co., 1965), 72.

12. C. S. Lewis, *The Abolition of Man* (New York: The Macmillan Co., 1947), 14.

13. Como, *Branches to Heaven,* 5.

14. Pitrim Sorokin, *The Crisis of Our Age* (New York: E. P. Dutton & Co., 1941), 205.

15. In Gibb, *Light on C. S. Lewis,* 61.

16. C. S. Lewis, *The Problem of Pain* (New York: Macmillan Co., 1962), 129.

17. C. S. Lewis, *The Allegory of Love* (New York: Oxford University Press, 1958), 330.

18. Lewis, *Abolition of Man,* 56.

19. Paul Holmer, *C. S. Lewis: The Shape of His Faith* (New York: Harper and Row, 1976), 62.

20. Lewis, "Poison of Subjectivism," in *Christian Reflections,* 73.

21. Lewis, "De Futilitate," in ibid., 66.

22. C. S. Lewis, *Spenser's Images of Life* (New York: Cambridge Universtiy Press, 1967), 68.

23. C. S. Lewis, *The Discarded Image* (Cambridge, England: Cambridge University Press, 1964), 157.

24. Gilbert Meilaender, *The Theory and Practice of Virtue* (Notre Dame, Ind.: University of Notre Dame Press, 1984), 68.

Chapter 1

1. C. S. Lewis, *Mere Christianity* (New York: Macmillan Co., 1943), 109.

2. C. S. Lewis, "Infatuation," in *Poems* (New York: Harcourt Brace Jovanovich, 1964), 75.

3. Tony Campolo, *The Seven Deadly Sins* (Dallas: Victor Books, 1989), 90.

4. Thomas Aquinas, *Summa Theologica,* II-II, 162, 1 (Benzinger Brothers Inc., Hyptertext Version Copyright © 1995, 1996 New Advent Inc.; www.newadvent.com).

5. *Sirach (Ecclesiasticus)* 10:12, *Good News Bible.* This "deuterocanonical" book formed part of the Septuagint—and the Latin Vulgate—used by medieval Christians.

6. C. S. Lewis, *The Great Divorce* (New York: Macmillan Co., 1946), 72.

7. C. S. Lewis, *The Magician's Nephew* (New York: Macmillan Co., 1955), 60.

8. Gilbert Meilaender, *Taste for the Other* (Grand Rapids: William B. Eerdmans Publishing Co., 1978), 46.

9. C. S. Lewis, ed., *George Macdonald: An Anthology,* by George Macdonald (Garden City, N.Y.: Doubleday and Co., 1962), 105.

10. Lewis, *Magician's Nephew,* 62, 18.

11. Lewis, *Mere Christianity,* 94.

12. Ibid., 35.

13. Ibid.

14. Ibid., 38.

15. Geoffrey Chaucer, "The Parson's Tale," in *The Canterbury Tales,* vol. 22 of *Great Books of the Western World* (Chicago: Encyclopedia Britannica, 1952), 23.

16. Lewis, *Problem of Pain,* 80.

17. Augustine, *The City of God,* XII, 8, in *Nicene and Post-Nicene Fathers,* 1st Ser., vol. 2 (Peabody, Mass.: Hendrickson Publishers Inc., 1995), 231.

18. Lewis, *Great Divorce,* 33.

19. C. S. Lewis, "Screwtape Proposes a Toast," in *The World's Last Night* (New York: Harcourt, Brace and World, 1960), 60.

20. Ibid.

21. Lewis, "Inner Ring," in *Weight of Glory,* 103.

22. Peter Kreeft, *Back to Virtue* (San Francisco: Ignatius Press, 1992), 100.

23. C. S. Lewis, *Perelandra* (New York: Macmillan Co., 1965), 96.

24. Kreeft, *Back to Virtue,* 100-101.

25. C. S. Lewis, "To a Lady," 9 July 1939, in W. H. Lewis, ed., *Letters of C. S. Lewis* (New York: Harcourt, Brace and World, 1966), 166-67.

26. This is the title of an enormously insightful book by American historian Carl Becker, who argues that Enlightenment thinkers replaced the "heavenly city" of Christian theology with humanly devised perfectionistic projects.

27. Lewis, *Pilgrim's Regress,* 35.

28. Lewis, *That Hideous Strength,* 41. (Feverstone earlier appeared as Divine, one of three space travelers to Malacandra in the first volume of the trilogy *Out of the Silent Planet*)

29. Ibid., 42.

30. Fyodor Mikhaylovich Dostoyevsky, *The Brothers Karamazov,* vol. 52 in *Great Books of the Western World* (Chicago: Encyclopedia Britannica, 1952), 11.

31. *The March of Freedom,* ed. Edwin A. Feulner (Dallas: Spence Publishing Co., 1998), 55.

32. Ibid.

Chapter 2

1. C. S. Lewis, *The Four Loves* (New York: Harcourt Brace Javanovich, 1960), 112.

2. Lewis, preface to *The Screwtape Letters* (New York: Time Inc., 1963), xxv.

3. Ibid.

4. Helmut Schoeck, *Envy: A Theory of Social Behaviour* (1969; reprint, Indianapolis: Liberty Fund, 1987), 116.

5. Aquinas, *Summa Theologica,* II-II, 36, 2.

6. Schoeck, *Envy,* 206-7.

7. C. S. Lewis, *The Last Battle* (New York: Macmillan Co., 1974), 147.

8. Chaucer, "The Parson's Tale," 516.

9. Hannah Arendt, *The Origins of Totalitarianism* (New York: Harcourt, Brace and Co., 1951), 438.

10. C. S. Lewis, "Equality," in *Present Concerns* (London: Harcourt Brace Jovanovich, 1986), 19.

11. Ibid., 20.

12. Lewis, "Screwtape Proposes a Toast," in *World's Last Night,* 60.

13. Lewis, "Democratic Education," in *Present Concerns,* 34.

14. Christina Hoff Sommers, a philosopher, distinguishes between "equity feminism," which rightly seeks "equal pay for equal work" and other such justice, and "gender feminism," which seeks to eradicate all sexual distinctions. Her treatise, *Who Stole Feminism? How Women Have Betrayed Women* (New York: Simon and Schuster, 1994), is one of the finest discussions of this issue.

15. Quoted in Charles Sykes, *A Nation of Victims* (New York: St. Martin's Press, 1992), 181.

16. Joyce Little, *The Church and the Culture War* (San Francisco: Ignatius Press, 1995), 76.

17. Lewis, "Equality," in *Present Concerns,* 19.

18. Danielle Crittenden, *What Our Mothers Didn't Tell Us: Why Happiness Eludes the Modern Woman* (New York: Simon and Schuster, 1999), 57.

19. Ibid., 141.

Chapter 3

1. Lewis, "Five Sonnets (1)," in *Poems,* 125.

2. Solomon Schimmel, *The Seven Deadly Sins* (New York: Oxford Univrsity Press, 1997), 83.

3. C. S. Lewis, *Letters to Malcolm: Chiefly on Prayer* (San Diego: Harcourt Brace Jovanovich, 1964), 97.

4. C. S. Lewis, *The Voyage of "The Dawn Treader"* (New York: Collier Books, 1952), 197.

5. Lewis, *Discarded Image,* 171.

6. Aristotle, *Nichomachean Ethics,* IV. v (New York: Penguin, 1953), 160.

7. Aquinas, *Summa Theologica,* II-II, 158, 1.

8. Ibid., Art. 2; also I-II, 21, 46-48.

9. Lewis, *Perelandra,* 155-56.

10. Lewis, *Last Battle,* 17.

11. Quoted in Gary B. Oliver, "The Power of Anger," *New Man,* September-October 1994, 62.

12. Aquinas, *Summa Theologica,* II-II, 158, 2.

13. Lewis, *Macdonald,* 35.

14. Lewis, *Great Divorce,* 35.

15. C. S. Lewis, *Till We Have Faces: A Myth Retold* (Grand Rapids: William B. Eerdmans Publishing Co., 1956), 148.

16. Ibid., 260.

17. Ibid.

18. Ibid.

19. Ibid., 266.

20. In *The Little Brown Book of Anecdotes,* ed. Clifton Fadiman (Boston: Little, Brown and Co., 1985), 298.

21. Lewis, *Great Divorce,* 95.

22. Lewis, *Last Battle,* 121.

23. Stephen Carter, *Civility: Manners, Morals, and the Etiquette of Democracy* (New York: HarperCollins, 1998), xii.

24. Ibid., 10-11.

25. Ibid., 38.

26. Ibid., 129.

27. In Fadiman, *Little Brown Book of Anecdotes,* 47.

28. C. S. Lewis, "Addison," in *Selected Literary Essays,* ed. Walter Hooper (Cambridge, England: Cambridge University Press, 1969), 156; the essay was published in 1946.

29. *The Practice of the Presence of God,*
www.ccel.org/b/bro_lawrence/practice/practice.html.

30. Carter, *Civility,* 31.

31. Ibid., 73.

32. Ibid., 259.

Chapter 4

1. C. S. Lewis, "Christianity and Culture," in *Christian Reflections,* 35.

2. Will Durant, *Our Oriental Heritage* (New York: Simon and Schuster, 1954), 44.

3. C. S. Lewis, *Surprised by Joy: The Shape of My Early Life* (San Diego: Harcourt, Brace and Co., 1955), 69.

4. Ibid., 45.

5. Ibid., 69.

6. Lewis, *Pilgrim's Regress,* 29.

7. Lewis, *Mere Christianity,* 89.

8. Dale Bruner, *The Christbook* (Waco: Word Books, 1987), 182.

9. William Barclay, *The Gospel of Matthew* (Philadelphia: Westminister Press, 1958), 144-45.

10. Augustine, *Sermon on the Mount,* in *Nicene and Post-Nicene Fathers,* 1st Series, vol. 6 (Peabody, Mass.: Hendrickson Publishers, 1995), 53.

11. John Chrysostom, *Homilies on The Gospel of Saint Matthew,* in ibid., 116.

12. *The Catechism of the Catholic Church* (Boston: St. Paul Books and Media, 1994), No. 2351, 564.

13. Lewis, *Mere Christianity,* 90.

14. Cristin Kellogg, "Couples: 'Sex Without Strings; Relationships Without Rings,'" *The Washington Times,* national edition, June 19-25, 2000, 17.

15. Wendy Shalit, *A Return to Modesty: Discovering the Lost Virtue* (New York: The Free Press, 1999).

16. Ibid., 107.

17. Ibid., 108.

18. Ibid., 235.

19. Ibid., 52.

20. Ibid., 6.

21. Ibid., 167.

22. Ibid., 8.

23. Michael Jones, *Degenerate Moderns: Modernity as Rationalized Sexual Misbehavior* (San Francisco: Ignatius Press, 1993), 11.

24. Ibid., 12.

25. Ibid., 17.

26. Quoted in Aquinas, *Summa Theologica,* II-II, Q. 153, Art. 1.

27. Ibid.

28. Jones, *Degenerate Moderns,* 181.

29. Sorokin, *Crisis of Our Age,* 19.

30. Ibid., 19.

31. Lewis, *Great Divorce,* 101.

32. Ibid., 102.

33. Ibid., 104-5.

Chapter 5

1. C. S. Lewis, *The Screwtape Letters* (Westwood, N.J.: Barbour Books, 1990), 89.

2. Lewis, "Some Thoughts," in *God in the Dock,* 149.

3. Aquinas, *Summa Theologica,* II-II, 148, 1.

4. Gregory I, *Moralia,* xxx, 18; cited in Ibid., II-II, 148, 4.

5. C. S. Lewis, *The Lion, the Witch, and the Wardrobe* (New York: Collier Books, 1950), 71.

6. Meilaender, *Taste for the Other,* 9.

7. Lewis, *The Silver Chair* (New York: Collier Books, 1953), 96.

8. Ibid., 99.

9. Virginia Stem Owens, "The Fatted Faithful," *Christianity Today,* January 11, 1999, 70.

10. Lewis, *Screwtape Letters* (Barbour Books), 86.

11. Ibid., 87.

12. Ibid.

13. Ibid.

14. Henry Fairlie, *The Seven Deadly Sins Today* (Notre Dame, Ind.: University of Notre Dame Press, 1979), 164.

15. Gregory I, *Moralia,* xxxi, 45.

16. Aquinas, *Summa Theologica,* II-II, 148, 6.

17. Lewis, *Silver Chair,* 151.

18. Ibid., 154.

19. Aquinas, *Summa Theologica,* II-II, 148, 6. He is citing 1 Esd. 3:20.

20. Ibid.

21. Lewis, *Abolition of Man,* 77.

22. Ibid., 78.

Chapter 6

1. C. S. Lewis, *Letters: C. S. Lewis/Don Giovanni Calabria* (Ann Arbor, Mich.: Servant Books, 1988), 10 September 1949, 55.

2. Quoted in Fairlie, *Deadly Sins,* 117.

3. Lewis, *Pilgrim's Regress,* 93.

4. Quoted in Fairlie, *Seven Deadly Sins,* 114; quoting her *The Other Six Deadly Sins,* I assume.

5. John of Damascus, *The Orthodox Faith,* II, in *Writings* (New York: Fathers of the Church, Inc., 1958).

6. Aquinas, *Summa Theologica,* II-II, 35, 1.

7. N. Scott Peck, *The Road Less Traveled* (New York: Simon and Schuster, 1978), 131.

8. Ibid., 272.

9. Ibid., 274.

10. Lewis, *Pilgrim's Regress,* 177.

11. Lewis, *Perelandra,* 36.

12. Ibid., 48.

13. Lewis, *Screwtape Letters* (Barbour Books), 11.

14. Ibid., 12.

15. Lewis, *Silver Chair,* 154.

16. Ibid., 157.

17. Ibid.

18. Ibid., 158.

19. Ibid., 1.

20. Ibid., 8.

21. "Harper's Index," *Harper's,* October 1990, 17.

22. Charles Sykes, *Dumbing Down Our Kids* (New York: St. Martin's Griffin, 1996), 100-101.

23. Lewis, *Letters,* 28 Mar 1921, 54.

24. Ibid.

25. Lewis, *Hideous Strength,* 185.

26. David Frum, *How We Got Here: The 70's: The Decade That Brought You Modern Life (For Better or Worse)* (New York: Basic Books, 2000), 157.

27. Marsha G. Witten, *All Is Forgiven: The Secular Message in American Protestantism* (Princeton, N.J.: Princeton University Press, 1993), 3.

28. Ibid., 44.

29. Ibid., 53.

30. Ibid., 132.

31. Ibid., 127.

Chapter 7

1. Lewis, *Pilgrim's Regress,* 177.

2. Aquinas, *Summa Theologica,* II-II, 118, 3.

3. Lewis, *George Macdonald,* 59.

4. Lewis, *Great Divorce,* 51.

5. Ibid.

6. Lewis, *Voyage of "The Dawn Treader,"* 105.

7. Ibid., 107.

8. Ibid., 108.

9. Lewis, *Pilgrim's Regress,* 80.

10. Lewis, *Screwtape Letters* (Barbour Books), 109.

11. Aquinas, *Summa Theologica,* II-II, 118, 1.

12. Lewis, *Surprised by Joy,* 9-10.

13. Lewis, *Voyage of "The Dawn Treader,"* 71.

14. Ibid.

15. Ibid., 71-72.

16. Lewis, *Abolition of Man,* 41.

17. Lewis, "The Inner Ring," in *Weight of Glory,* 104.

18. Quoted in "Reflections," *Christianity Today,* June 12, 2000, 89.

Chapter 8

1. Lewis, *Mere Christianity,* 74-75.

2. Ravi Zacharias, *Deliver Us from Evil* (Dallas: Word Publishing Co., 1996), 140.

3. William Bennett, *Body Count* (New York: Simon and Schuster, 1996), 56.

4. Lewis, *Lion, Witch, and Wardrobe,* 44.

5. Ibid., 45.

6. Lewis, *Pilgrim's Regress,* 61.

7. Ibid., 62.

8. Lewis, *Discarded Image,* 154; citing *Canterbury Tales,* I, 262.

9. Ibid., 158.

10. Ibid.

11. Ibid.

12. Ibid., 160.

13. Lewis, *Miracles* (London: Geoffrey Bles, 1966), 14.

14. Ibid.

15. Ibid., 34.

16. Ibid., 35.

17. As cited in Aquinas, *Summa Theologica,* II-II, 47, 1.

18. Quoted in Pieper, *Four Virtues* (Notre Dame, Ind.: University of Notre Dame Press, 1966), 4.

19. Ibid., 7.

20. Aristotle, *Nichomachean Ethics,* 209.

21. Ibid., 330-31.

22. Pieper, *Four Virtues,* 15.

23. Lewis, *Voyage of "The Dawn Treader,"* 146.

24. Lewis, *Screwtape Letters* (Barbour Books), 126

25. Ibid., 130.

26. Ibid., 139.

27. Ibid., 140.

28. Quoted in R. L. Green and Walter Hooper, *C. S. Lewis: A Biography* (London: Collins Fount, 1979), 129.

29. Pieper, *Four Virtues,* 4.

30. Ibid., 53.

31. Ibid., 54.

32. Ibid., 9.

33. Lewis, *Hideous Strength,* 145.

34. Ibid., 144.

35. Lewis, *Miracles,* 39.

36. Carter, *Civility,* 288-89.

Chapter 9

1. C. S. Lewis, *A Preface to Paradise Lost* (London: Oxford University Press, 1960), 74.

2. Lewis, *The Last Battle,* 16-17.

3. Ibid., 17.

4. Ibid., 24.

5. Ibid.

6. Ibid.

7. Plato, "Gorgias," in *The Dialogues of Plato* (New York: Bantam Books, 1986), 338.

8. *Justicia est ad alterum,* to cite the familiar Latin maxim.

9. Aristotle, *Nichomachean Ethics,* V, 5.

10. Aquinas, *Summa Theologica,* II-II, 58, i.

11. Pieper, *Four Virtues,* 58.

12. Lewis, *Mere Christianity,* 82.

13. Lewis, *That Hideous Strength,* 13.

14. Ibid., 151.

15. Ibid.

16. Lewis, "The Humanitarian Theory of Punishment," in *God in the Dock,* III, 4, 500.

17. Ibid.

18. Ibid., 499.

19. Ibid.

20. Lewis, *Mere Christianity,* 70-71.

21. Augustine, *The Epistle of St. John,* in *Nicene and Post-Nicene Fathers of the Christian Church,* First Series, VII (Grand Rapids: William B. Eerdmans Publishing Co., 1986), 505.

22. Lewis, *Preface to Paradise Lost,* 74.

23. Lewis, "Membership," in *Weight of Glory,* 115-16.

24. Pieper, *Four Virtues,* 102-3.

25. Lewis, "Democratic Education," in *Present Concerns,* 33.

26. Irving Kristol, *Neoconservatism* (New York: The Free Press, 1995), 167.

27. Pieper, *Four Virtues,* 81.

28. Ibid., 89.

29. Ibid., 91.

30. Lewis, "Kipling's World," in *Selected Literary Essays,* 240.

31. Lewis, "To Mrs. Edward A. Allen," in *The Letters of C. S. Lewis,* 1 February 1958, 281.

32. Balint Vazsonyi, *America's 30 Years War: Who Is Winning?* (Washington, D.C.: Regnery Publishing, 1998).

33. Ibid., 13.

34. Ibid., 53.

35. Ibid., 57-58.

36. Ibid., 176-77.

Chapter 10

1. Lewis, *Mere Christianity,* 76.

2. Aquinas, *Summa Theologica,* II-II, 123, 1.

3. Lewis, *Screwtape Letters* (Barbour Books), 143.

4. Aquinas, *Summa Theologica,* II-II, Q. 123, Art. 6.

5. Lewis, *Screwtape Letters* (Barbour Books), 148-49.

6. Aleksandr Solzhenitsyn, *A World Split Apart* (New York: Harper and Row, 1978), 9-10.

7. Lewis, *Abolition of Man,* 35.

8. William Shakespeare, *Julius Caesar,* II, ii, 32.

9. Lewis, *Perelandra,* 142.

10. Ibid., 147.

11. Ibid., 156.

12. Lewis, *Screwtape Letters,* 106.

13. Aquinas, *Summa Theologica,* II-II, 123, 4.

14. Lewis, *Abolition of Man,* 119.

15. Pieper, *Four Virtues,* 132.

16. Lewis, *Present Concerns,* 13.

17. Ibid.

18. Ibid.

19. Ibid.

20. Pieper, *Four Virtues,* 130.

21. Lewis, *Present Concerns,* 15.

22. Lewis, *Last Battle,* 121.

23. Lewis, *Prince Caspian* (New York: Collier Books, 1970), 189.

24. Lewis, *Lion, Witch, and Wardrobe,* 127-28.

25. Ibid., 129.

26. Lewis, *Prince Caspian,* 74.

27. Ibid., 75.

28. Ibid.

29. Ibid., 203.

30. *The C. S. Lewis Readers' Encyclopedia* (Grand Rapids: Zondervan Publishing House, 1998), 418.

31. Lewis, *Voyage of "The Dawn Treader,"* 27.

32. Ibid., 28.

33. Address at Harrow School, October 29, 1941, in Stephen Mansfield, *Never Give In: The Extraordinary Character of Winston Churchill* (Elkton, Md.: Highland Press, 1995), 142.

34. Margaret Thatcher, *The Downing Street Years* (New York: HarperCollins, 1994), 167.

Chapter 11

1. Lewis, *Weight of Glory,* 3.

2. Thucydides, *The Peloponnesian War,* vol. VI in *Great Books of the Western World,* I, iii, 4.

3. Tom Landry, with Gregg Lewis, *An Autobiography* (Grand Rapids: Zondervan Publishing House, 1990), 276.

4. William Bennett, John J. DiIulio Jr., and John P. Walters, *Body Count* (New York: Simon and Schuster, 1996), 208.

5. Lewis, *Preface to Paradise Lost,* 81.

6. Augustine, *De Morib. Eccl. xix.,* quoted in Aquinas, *Summa Theologica,* II-II, 141, 2.

7. Lewis, *Mere Christianity,* 61.

8. This translation appears in Pieper's *Four Virtues.*

9. Lewis, *Pilgrim's Regress,* 86.

10. Ibid.

11. Ibid.

12. Aquinas, *Summa Theologica,* II-II, 141, 1.

13. Pieper, *Four Virtues,* 148.

14. Ibid., 151.

15. Ibid., 160.

16. Lewis, *Mere Christianity,* 75.

17. Lewis, *Perelandra,* 42.

18. Ibid.

19. Ibid., 48.

20. Lewis, "The Necessity of Chivalry," in *Present Concerns,* 14.

21. Ibid., 15.

22. Lewis, *Letters to An American Lady* (Grand Rapids: William B. Eerdmans, 1967), 35.

23. Lewis, *Last Battle,* 120-21.

24. Ibid., 121.

25. Lewis, "The Necessity of Christianity," in *Present Concerns,* 13, 15.

26. Aeschlishman, *Restitution of Man,* 75.

27. *Lewis, Hideous Strength,* 296.

28. Quoted by Green and Hooper, *C. S. Lewis,* 173.

29. Lewis, "De Descriptione Temporum," in *Selected Literary Essays,* 10.

Chapter 12

1. Lewis, *Mere Christianity,* 129.

2. Lewis, "De Descriptione Temporum," in *Selected Literary Essays,* 11.

3. Quoted in Joseph Pieper, *Faith, Hope, Love* (San Francisco: Ignatius Press, 1997), 57.

4. Lewis, *Silver Chair,* 21.

5. Ibid., 146.

6. Quoted by John Paul II, *Fides et Ratio* (Boston: Pauline Books and Media, 1998), 79.

7. Aquinas, *Summa Theologica,* II-II, 2, xx.

8. Lewis, *Miracles,* 76.

9. George Orwell, *1984* (New York: New American Library, 1962), 205.

10. Peter Kreeft and Ronald K. Tacelli, *Handbook of Christian Apologetics: Hundreds of Answers to Crucial Questions* (Downers Grove, Ill.: Inter-Varsity Press, 1994), 363.

11. Ibid.

12. Lewis, "On the Obstinacy in Belief," in *The World's Last Night,* 17-18.

13. Lewis, "Transposition," in *Weight of Glory,* 70.

14. George Weigel, "Holy Land Pilgrimage: A Diary," *First Things,* June—July 2000, 27.

15. A. W. Tozer, *The Incredible Christian* (Harrisburg, Pa.: Christian Publications, 1964), 27.

16. Diogenes Allen, *Christian Belief in a Postmodern World: The Full Wealth of Conviction* (Louisville: Westminister/John Knox Press, 1989), 1.

17. Lewis, "Modern Man and His Categories of Thought," in *Present Concerns,* 65.

18. Allen, *Christian Belief,* 155.

19. Lewis, "On the Obstinacy of Belief," in *The World's Last Night,* 29-30.

20. Lewis, "Religion: Reality or Substitute?" in *Christian Reflections,* 42.

21. Lewis, "On the Obstinacy in Belief," 23.

22. Ibid.

23. Oswald Chambers, *My Utmost for His Highest* (Ulrichsville, Ohio: Barbour and Co., 1963), 189.

Chapter 13

1. Lewis, *Weight of Glory,* 7.

2. Lewis, *Surprised by Joy,* 63.

3. C. S. Lewis, *A Grief Observed* (1961; reprint, New York: Bantam Books, 1976), 4.

4. Ibid., 5.

5. Ibid., 25.

6. Ibid., 49.

7. Aquinas, *Summa Theologica,* II-II, 17, 2.

8. Ibid.

9. Augustine, quoted in Pieper, *Faith, Hope, Love,* 113.

10. Aquinas, *Summa Theologica,* II-II, 20, 3.

11. Ibid., 113.

12. Ibid., II-II, 21, 1.

13. Ibid.

14. Lewis, *Problem of Pain,* 128.

15. Lewis, "The Trouble with X," in *God in the Dock,* 155.

16. Lewis, *Preface to Paradise Lost,* 104-5.

17. Lewis, *Mere Christianity,* 106.

18. Quoted in Pieper, *Faith, Hope, Love,* 111.

19. Ibid.

20. Lewis, *Great Divorce,* 104-5.

21. "Don v. Devil," *Time,* September 8, 1947, 66.

22. Lewis, *Miracles,* 162-163.

23. Lewis, *Great Divorce,* 68-69.

24. Lewis, *Problem of Pain,* 144.

25. Ibid.

26. Ibid., 145.

27. Lewis, *Voyage of "The Dawn Treader,"* 199.

28. Ibid.

29. Ibid., 213.

30. Lewis, *The Last Battle,* 171.

31. Lewis, *Weight of Glory,* 6.

32. Ibid., 18.

Chapter 14

1. C. S. Lewis, *Letters to Children,* ed. Lyle W. Dorsett and Marjorie Lamp Mead (New York: Macmillan Co., 1985), October 26, 1963, 111.

2. Lewis, *Four Loves,* 13.

3. Lewis, *Pilgrim's Regress,* 177.

4. Lewis, *Four Loves,* 163.

5. Ibid., 20-21.

6. Lewis, *George Macdonald,* 32.

7. Lewis, *Problem of Pain,* 40.

8. Pieper, *Faith, Hope, Love,* 87.

9. Augustine, *First Epistle of St. John,* 505.

10. Lewis, *Great Divorce,* 94.

11. Ibid., 92-93.

12. Ibid., 93.

13. Lewis, *Four Loves,* 169.

14. Quoted in Pieper, *Faith, Hope, Love,* 168.

15. Lewis, *Four Loves,* 32.

16. Pieper, *Faith, Hope, Love,* 174.

17. Lewis, *Letters to an American Lady,* 18 Aug 1956, 61.

18. Quoted in Vincent Rossi, "Theocentrism: The Cornerstone of Christian Ecology," in *Ecology and Life,* ed. Wes Granberg-Michaelson (Dallas: Word Publishing, 1988), 159.

19. Lewis's letter, 10 Jan 1931, in George Sayer, *Jack: A Life of C. S. Lewis* (Wheaton, Ill.: Crossway Books, 1994), 246.

20. Ibid., 248.

21. C. S. Lewis, *Letters to Malcolm* (London: Geoffrey Bles, 1964), 75.

22. Lewis, *Mere Christianity,* 117.

23. Lewis, *Four Loves,* 53.

24. Ibid., 76.

25. Ibid., 134.

26. Ibid., 158.

27. Ibid., 184.